667

D1156217

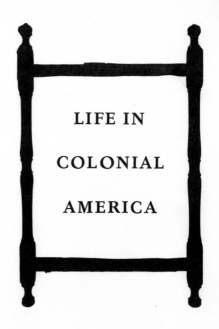

LIFE IN

COLONIAL

AMERICA

Art Work by Charles Walker

together with numerous old prints

A CHANTICLEER PRESS EDITION

LIFE IN
COLONIAL
AMERICA

ELIZABETH GEORGE SPEARE

RANDOM HOUSE

Acknowledgments

The publishers would like to express their deep appreciation to
the following organizations and individuals who were particularly
helpful during the preparation of this book:

Brooklyn Museum (Robert Riley) for advice on costume.

Colonial Williamsburg (Robert W. Jeffrey) for numerous
photographs and for criticism of art work.

Free Library of Philadelphia (Miss Ellen Shaffer) for help in
selecting illustrations from rare children's books.

Library of Congress (Miss Alice Lee Parker and Milton Kaplan)
for guidance in finding original prints and drawings.

New-York Historical Society (Richard J. Koke) for photographs
and for checking certain illustrations.

Old Sturbridge Village for photographs of everyday objects in
New England and for checking of art work.

"The staff of Plimoth Plantation" for information on life in early
Massachusetts.

Gratitude is also due to the following institutions which rendered
valuable assistance:

Bostonian Society; Jamestown Foundation; Mariners Museum,
Newport News; Massachusetts Historical Society; Mount Vernon Ladies'
Association of the Union; Nantucket Historical Association; Saugus
Iron Works Association, Saugus, Mass.; Whaling Museum, New
Bedford, Mass.; Westpoint Museum and the Winchester Gun Museum.

© 1963 by Random House, Inc.

*All rights reserved under International and Pan-American
Copyright Conventions. Published in New York by Random House, Inc.,
and simultaneously in Toronto, Canada, by Random House of Canada, Ltd.*

PLANNED AND PRODUCED BY CHANTICLEER PRESS, INC., NEW YORK

Library of Congress Catalog Card Number: 63—11951
Manufactured in the United States of America

Contents

North Haven Memorial Library
North Haven, Conn.

32887

Plantation Life

I

On a fine spring morning a small band of gentlemen in velvet doublets and plumed hats climbed from their boat to the bank of a river in Virginia. All about them they saw "fair meadows and goodly tall trees, with fresh water running through." Weary from almost five months at sea, impatient to begin searching for the gold they were certain lay close at hand, they decided to look no further. Here they would build their town. They carried back word to the three ships anchored in the river, where the rest of the company, one hundred and five in all, waited with impatience to begin their venture in the New World. On the same day, they broke ground for what was to be the first permanent settlement in America, calling it Jamestown in honor of His Majesty King James of England. It was May of 1607, thirteen years before the *Mayflower* carried another band of settlers to northern Plymouth.

The Jamestown Colony Survives

The new land soon proved to be far from paradise. There was no gold. Instead there were mosquitoes, heat, malaria, hunger, and most dismaying of all, endless hard work. The adventurers were unused to labor and ridiculously clothed for it; some of the men had even brought starch for the ruffs that bedecked their fine doublets. Disappointed and resentful, they abandoned their daydreams in a wretched struggle for existence. In the next few years the Jamestown experiment might have ended in failure but for the fortunate arrival of a shipload of new settlers, who brought with them renewed life and hope.

There was no ease or luxury for these first colonists. A terrifying Indian attack showed them that their immediate need was a stockade for

Palisaded against Indian attacks, Jamestown (facing page) was a tight community of homes, church, guardhouse, and storehouse. The soldiers at the gate (above) were dressed and armed like English foot soldiers.

protection, and they set to work to erect a triangular fort of upright poles, with a bulwark at each corner on which they mounted their small cannon. For their first shelters they threw together wigwams of branches or crude tents. As rapidly as possible they had to clear the thickly forested land. Meanwhile they planted their first corn wherever they could find a few feet of soil and sunshine.

The first houses were one-room cabins of boards standing upright in the ground, with roofs of thatch. A few, more permanent structures were of logs, squared and fitted together, or nailed with homemade wooden pegs, for iron nails were so scarce that if a man moved or built a new house he burned down his old one just to salvage the nails. The chinks between the rough planks were stuffed with moss or "wattle and daub" made from mud and straw. A door of a double layer of thick planks was set on wooden hinges and heavily barred within. If there were a window at all, it was small and high, with a rough bark shutter, and it was filled with paper soaked in linseed oil, which let in only the palest glimmer of light. Because of the warm climate the Southern settlers placed their chimneys at one end of their houses, building them out from the wall to reduce the danger of fire.

The furniture in these early houses was of the simplest sort. The settlers brought with them almost nothing but the chests which contained their clothing. Whatever they needed had to be hewn from the forest. Oaken boards set on trestles made a long table for eating and could be removed when the meal was done. The head of the house might make a sturdy chair for himself; the rest of the family sat on stools or benches. Clothing hung on pegs along the wall. In one corner stood the large bed, an elaborate affair even in the simplest cabin, for the English settlers were used to sleeping behind heavy curtains. A cupboard with the wooden plates and trenchers used at meals, the kettles for cooking, the spinning wheel, and a matchlock rifle made up the remaining furnishings. Candles were the only light.

Before long the most enterprising of the settlers discovered the crop that was to transform their miserable settlement into a thriving colony. The fertile soil of Virginia proved to be ideal for the raising of tobacco, a weed which Spanish explorers had discovered in America and introduced into England, where it was in great demand among people of fashion. John Rolfe, the middle-aged and romantic gentleman who fell in love with and married the Indian princess Pocahontas, was among the first to perfect a sweet-leafed variety and a secret method of curing it. In a very few years ships laden with tobacco were sailing from Virginia.

From small experiments at Jamestown came the South's major industry— tobacco raising. (New- York Historical Society)

The men who set about tobacco-raising in earnest were not the would-be gentlemen and adventurers, but new settlers of stamina and determination. Because tobacco crops required much land, they did not group their farms close together, but spread them out along the banks of the river at some distance from each other. There they began a lonely, hard-working existence.

Bond Servants and Slaves

In far less time than was possible in the Northern settlements the life of the Virginia planters became easier. The climate was in their favor, and they presently solved even the problem of the hard work. By a special order of the king, one hundred convicts were sent from the prisons of England to be sold as servants to the planters. For the next hundred years many shiploads of such laborers poured into the colonies.

The laws of England were brutally severe. A man could be hanged for stealing a loaf of bread, and most of these convicts were desperately poor men, grateful to escape the gallows and to have a chance in the New World. Their chances were not always much to be grateful for. They were bonded to planters, usually for five years, to cover the cost of their passage. During that time they were the property of their owner, to be fed, worked, clothed and punished as their owners were inclined. Many of

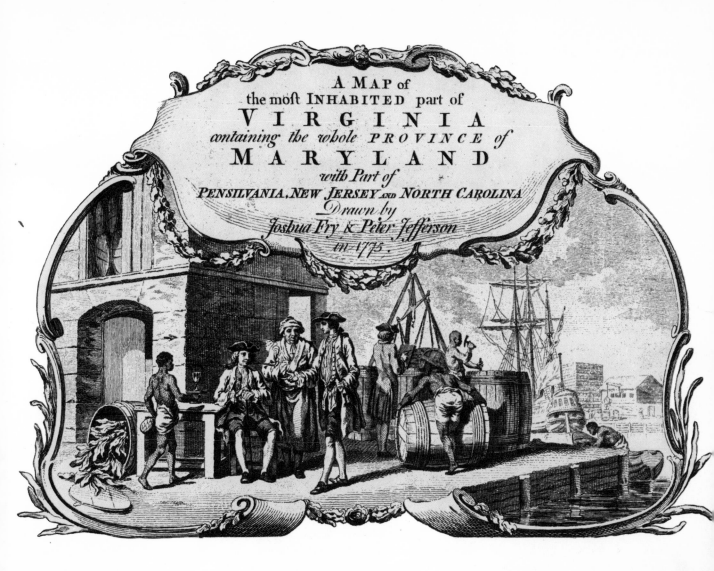

A MAP of the moſt INHABITED part of VIRGINIA containing the whole PROVINCE of MARYLAND with Part of PENSILVANIA, NEW JERSEY AND NORTH CAROLINA Drawn by Joshua Fry & Peter Jefferson in 1775.

them fared miserably and finished their time of servitude in such a destitute condition that they were forced to sell themselves for another term to stay alive. But many managed to acquire a small plot of land of their own, and at the end of their terms became independent settlers.

In 1619 a Dutch trading vessel brought from Africa to Jamestown a cargo of twenty Negroes, who were sold to the planters as bond servants on the same terms as the English convicts. A few managed to work out their terms and attain their freedom. But most of them, helpless, bewildered, ignorant of white men's ways, proved either rebellious or "lazy." Soon Negro slaves became by law the property of an owner for life, to be reckoned as real estate like his land or his horses.

Slave trading became a profitable business. Sea captains purchased shiploads of slaves from African slave drivers and brought them to America chained between the decks, where many of them died during the passage. In Virginia they were bought by dealers, washed, fed and clothed to make a presentable appearance, and driven, usually in leg-irons, to some central point where they were sold at a public auction. Slaves who had worked for a long time for one master were sometimes sold off in the same way. A few dealers made an attempt to keep families together,

Slaves roll hogsheads of tobacco from their master's wharf to a waiting vessel.

but often wives were separated from their husbands, and children from their mothers. In the tobacco fields they were put to the heaviest kind of work, with no hope of ever gaining their freedom.

A Little Town in Itself

New plantations and towns spread rapidly along the James River for a hundred miles. As a settler prospered he would buy more acres to add to his original farm, or move to a new location, for tobacco soon exhausted the soil. Now he would be dissatisfied with his old frame house. There must be a two-story house, rectangular, with dormer windows in the sloping roof, and a chimney at either end. The new house might even be of brick. The walls within might be plastered with clay, whitened by lime, and there would be casement windows, opening outward like small doors, with diamond-shaped panes set in leaden frames, the glass imported from England. The crude handmade furniture would be replaced now with tables and chairs, also ordered from England. The wooden tableware would be replaced by pewter, a silvery metal made from tin mixed with

Gingerbread men, shaped in the hand-carved cooky mold at right, were transferred to a metal sheet for baking. (Colonial Williamsburg)

lead. A family might add silver, spoons and dishes bought piece by piece, for in those days to own silver was like having money in the bank.

As a man's tobacco crop prospered, his plantation house became larger and more luxurious. The old house might be converted into a kitchen, and servants would carry the food in covered dishes to the dining room in the new house. There would be other small buildings for the spinning and weaving and laundering required by his growing household. Unlike the Northern farmer, the Southern colonist could not count on his neighbors for help. The nearest plantation might be miles away. There were no convenient shops where he could purchase shoes for himself or for his horse, or a new bonnet for his wife. He needed to have right on his own farm the means of meeting almost all his needs. The few articles and luxuries he could not produce for himself came to him from England, often on his own ship that sailed up the river right to his private wharf.

All this meant that as a man prospered he added to his household more and more slaves. A large plantation kept hundreds of slaves busy. There were unskilled field hands, including women and children. There were trusted house servants. There were other slaves trained as carpenters and weavers and shoemakers and blacksmiths and furniture makers and cooks. All these slaves labored from morning till night, and slept crowded into miserable cabins or "slave quarters" out of sight of the house. On George Washington's estate at Mount Vernon, for example, there was a smithy, a brick-making kiln, a flour mill, a smokehouse for curing meat over a wood fire, a spinning and weaving house, as well as henhouses, stables, barns, cottages for white servants and extensive slave quarters.

In time this sprawling, self-sustaining plantation became a little town in itself. And of all this busy community the owner was master and lord. One writer has pointed out that the mayor of a town, the judge, the sheriff and the preacher, all combined, were not so powerful as a plantation owner. He planned and supervised the daily work, he alone maintained law and order, and he alone reaped all the benefits.

Stately Mansions and Manners

By the eighteenth century there were many large and wealthy plantations, not only in Virginia but also in Maryland and the Carolinas. Their owners lived in some of the most beautiful houses ever built anywhere, large and handsome, with vast lawns and gardens. These houses, called Georgian after the English kings of that period, were carefully designed so that the doors and windows, the wings, even the kitchens and other outbuildings were all planned to make one harmonious design. A typical Southern version of the Georgian house was Mount Vernon, with its portico or porch and its stately white columns. Another famous mansion was Westover, built by William Byrd, a wealthy Virginian. This was a fine brick structure, spacious and beautifully proportioned.

Inside such houses as Westover, gleaming mahogany furniture reflected the candlelight from crystal chandeliers. Oriental rugs, tapestries, mirrors and paintings glowed on paneled walls. Harpsichords and other musical instruments waited the guests' pleasure in the drawing rooms. Silver and gold dishes of lavish size graced the dining rooms—cups and plates and wine bowls, and even huge punch bowls engraved with the family coat of arms.

The men and women who moved gracefully through the great rooms

A shoo-fly chair, worked by a foot pedal.

13

Mount Vernon, home of George Washington, showing a typical plantation with mansion, outbuildings, elaborate gardens, and a private wharf.

of such houses, and strolled about the smooth lawns and formal gardens, looked very different from their sturdily clad grandparents. Sailing ships from England brought the finest and richest of brocades and satins and damasks, laces and perfumes. Men strutted in velvet or satin waistcoats encrusted with embroidered flowers. Styles veered about according to the latest London fashion, with coats now full-skirted, now straight, but whatever the cut, they were all made of the most elegant materials and adorned with elaborate embroidery, double rows of gold buttons, and lace and ruffles. Knee-length breeches were carefully fitted to display a well-turned leg. Stockings were of white silk, held up by velvet garters. Shoes tilted on red heels, and were ornamented by glittering paste buckles. Hat brims became so wide that they had to be tacked up, first on one side, then on the other, and finally on three sides, when they became the famous three-cornered "cocked hats," handsomely decorated with gold braid.

Right: A silver-handled razor, imported from Europe. (Colonial Williamsburg)

Below: A curling iron used sizzling hot.

Women swayed and rustled haughtily, and breathed daintily against the whalebone stays that bound their tiny waists. Low-cut bodices and short sleeves were softened by delicate falls of lawn and lace. Outer skirts were looped back to reveal petticoats of brilliant silk, and great hoop frames ballooned these billowing petticoats to a width of four feet. Two ladies in such skirts could barely fit into a coach, and a special chair with cut-off arms had to be devised to accommodate them.

Colonial ladies delighted in accessories. There were tiny patchboxes of silver or ivory or tortoise shell, with little mirrors inside the lids to aid in placing exactly the tiny black "beauty spots" that would show off a creamy skin. When a lady rode abroad this same complexion was protected from the sun and air by a linen or velvet mask. There were dainty lace and silk handkerchiefs, ribbon girdles, gold and silver buckles and clasps, gold rings and lockets. To a Southern lady her fan was indispensable, and at balls she toyed with an exquisite fan of carved ivory or peacock feathers. From her waist swung a little etui, or ornamental bag, which carried small scissors, thread, and other feminine notions.

In our day husbands joke about their wives' hats, but in this matter colonial ladies were less fanciful than men. They contented themselves with simple hoods. Philip Fithian, a young Northerner who spent a year in Virginia as a tutor on a wealthy plantation, once wrote in his journal:

> *. . . it is a custom among the . . . ladies, whenever they go from home, to muffle up their heads and necks, leaving only a narrow passage for the eyes, in cotton or silk handkerchiefs; I was in distress for them when I first came into the colony, for every woman that I saw abroad I looked upon as ill either with the mumps or toothache!*

But any hat would have been impossible over some of the hairdos that women wore during the eighteenth century. They pulled their hair high into towering creations, rolled over little silk cushions and carefully powdered. It took hours for a hairdresser to perfect such a work of art, and to preserve it as long as possible a woman had to sleep on a wooden block instead of a pillow. Wigs, when they came in style, were almost as uncomfortable, but could at least be removed at night.

Men could not criticize such hairdos because for nearly a hundred years they themselves put up with the nuisance and expense and discomfort of wigs. Their wigs changed styles many times, all the way from long curly periwigs to puffy white wigs with long braids hanging down the back. They were hot and heavy and uncomfortable. They cost as much as ten pounds and needed to be constantly sent to the hairdresser for curling and dressing. At one time men added to the discomfort by powdering their wigs with a white chalky powder which was choking to apply and which drifted untidily over their fine waistcoats. Even after they abandoned wigs, men continued to powder their natural hair. Just before the Revolution plainer dress became patriotic, and men began to wear their hair in simple queues tied in the back with a ribbon.

The Master of Westover

William Byrd, owner of Westover, kept a careful journal of his life from day to day. As we read it we can see that the life of a plantation owner was not one of carefree ease. Every day Byrd made the rounds of his estate, supervising all the work from the planting of young trees to the

To protect himself from the powder dusted freely over his wig, a gentleman breathes through a paper cone.

unloading of a ship of provisions. He looked over the harvest of tobacco and watched the shearing of sheep. On occasion he lent a hand himself.

The journal is filled with the many troubles which vexed a plantation owner. His slaves were continually running away. His overseers were dishonest. His crops were spoiled by heavy rains. His pigs and sheep wandered into his neighbor's fields and caused hard feeling. His mill dam broke and flooded his land. Fevers and mysterious illnesses spread through the slaves' quarters and threatened his own children. And despite the vast wealth that tobacco brought, he seems always to have had a struggle to make both ends meet. The Virginia planters never had the thrift of the New Englanders and Dutch, and their elaborate way of life was often far beyond their means.

Byrd was constantly called upon to doctor some ailing slave, and one shudders to read of the bitter concoctions his slaves were forced to down. Bloodletting, which meant drawing a small amount of blood from the veins, was a popular cure of the day, and Byrd prescribed it for almost any complaint—for headache, a pain in the side, a sore throat, or a fall from a horse.

Discipline at Westover seems to have been strict but not harsh, and Byrd's journal is an illustration of the attitude of the most humane owners. There was no law to curb a brutal master and no one could interfere, even if he drove his slaves to death. But William Byrd prided himself on the fair treatment of his slaves. At times he was even indulgent, but at other times he seems shockingly indifferent. On one morning he quarreled with his wife for beating her maid with the tongs, yet he seemingly objected only to her unladylike display of temper. He ordered any number of whippings—for laziness, for not writing well, for drinking the rum and filling the bottle with water.

Advertisements like this one from the "Virginia Gazette" of 1767 were not uncommon. Generally they did not go so far as to advertise for slaves dead or alive.
(Colonial Williamsburg)

RUN AWAY from the subscriber in *Norfolk*, about the 20th of *October* last, two young Negro fellows, *viz.* WILL, about 5 feet 8 inches high, middling black, well made, is an outlandish fellow, and when he is surprised the white of his eyes turns red; I bought him of Mr. *Moss*, about 8 miles below *York*, and imagine he is gone that way, or some where between *York* and *Williamsburg*. PETER, about 5 feet 9 inches high, a very black slim fellow, has a wife at *Little Town*, and a father at Mr. *Philip Burt's* quarter, near the half-way house between *Williamsburg* and *York*; he formerly belonged to Parson *Fontaine*, and I bought him of Doctor *James Carter*. They are both outlawed; and TEN POUNDS a piece offered to any person that will kill the said Negroes, and bring me their heads, or THIRTY SHILLINGS for each if brought home alive.
JOHN BROWN.

Of course, everywhere in colonial America whipping was the common punishment, and even doting parents felt it their duty to beat the slightest hint of wickedness out of their offspring. Slaves, who were ignorant and unpaid, could be even more ornery than children, and owners did not

At a slave auction, men, women, and children were sold like livestock to the highest bidders.

know any other way to keep them working. A slave who was quick and industrious was rewarded by special privileges. Byrd wrote on several occasions of sending treats of cider to the slaves' quarters, and he was careful not to make them work too much on Sunday. One day he wrote, "In the evening we were merry with nonsense, and so were my servants."

Young Masters and Mistresses

The boys who grew up on these plantations, especially the eldest sons who would one day be masters, had to learn all the complicated business of management. They did not go to school like boys in New England. Because the settlements were so far apart, there were few public schools in Virginia. Wealthy parents engaged tutors for their sons or sent them to England for their education. On the smaller farms an educated bond servant sometimes served as teacher for the children of the family. Occasionally a charitable master even saw to it that his slaves' children learned to read and write, but most owners considered this a waste of time.

More valuable than the Latin he learned from his tutors was the practical management a boy picked up from observing the work of the plantation. Arithmetic and bookkeeping he learned at the plantation store, along with shrewd bargaining. Every detail of the tobacco trade he observed from the time he could walk. He saw how the men protected the tender plants from worms and suckers and weeds, how they cut the stalks and hung and graded and cured them and pressed them into large barrels called hogsheads. He would never do this work himself, but he must know when it was done well or poorly. Most important of all, he learned to be a master of men, and it is not surprising that many of the great leaders of the new American republic received their boyhood education on the Southern plantations.

In the same way the daughters of the master learned the management of a great house. A Virginia lady once wrote: "Very little from books was thought necessary for a girl. She was trained to domestic matters, however, must learn the accomplishments of the day, to play upon the harpsichord or spinet, and to work impossible dragons and roses on canvas." In short, she must learn to be a lady, which was no easy matter. She must understand all the intricate processes of spinning and weaving and cooking in order to recognize and demand the best in her own household, for the mistress of a plantation had many responsibilities. She had to supervise the cooking and clothmaking for her family and servants and slaves, and all the countless details that kept the vast household running smoothly. On her fell the burden of the lavish entertaining for which the plantations were famous.

Martha Washington, in addition to being a thrifty and capable manager, had a reputation as a charming hostess. Her needlework was a source of pride to her family. During the lean years of the Revolution she set an example for colonial women by weaving cloth for her own gowns from thread carefully raveled from her husband's silk stockings and some discarded damask chair covers. William Byrd's wife, on the contrary, was less of a helpmeet, frequently ailing and inclined to make a fuss over trifles. On one occasion he wrote in his diary:

> *My wife and I quarrelled about her pulling her brows. She threatened she would not go to Williamsburg if she might not pull them; I refused, however, and got the better of her and maintained my authority.*

The Tradition of Hospitality

Such a trip as the Byrds' visit to Williamsburg was a rarity. It required infinite preparation and a tiring journey over atrocious roads. For the most part, entertainment had to be provided on the plantation. The men enjoyed hunting and fishing, card-playing, and conversation over endless dishes of tea. Byrd sometimes played a game of cards with his wife to amuse her, and in the evening would walk with her in the garden. Without visitors, life on a plantation was dull, and a ready welcome awaited anyone who came to the door. "There came an abundance of people to

Hand-painted on this fan are the surrender of a fortress, a naval battle, and a cavalry engagement. (Metropolitan Museum of Art)

A guitar, made in England in 1764. (Colonial Williamsburg)

*As in England, the minuet was a
popular dance at fashionable balls.*

visit us," William Byrd often wrote, and we may be sure that a laden table and flowing cups celebrated their coming. Food on the plantations was overabundant and elegantly served. There was fresh fish from the river, wild game and beef, mutton and poultry. Peaches and pears and apples hung ripe on the trees, and walnuts and hickory nuts and chestnuts clustered on the ground. Cooks took pride in turning out a rich sauce or a delicate pudding. The reader of Byrd's diary finds his mouth watering at mention of roast pigeon, wild duck, blue-wing pie, asparagus, strawberries and cherries. There was a well-stocked wine cellar, and when company arrived the huge silver bowl overflowed with sillabub, a frothy concoction of wine and cream. Visitors did not have to be specially invited. A stranger on horseback or a trader sailing up the river, anyone who might bring news of the outside world or a bit of lively gossip, was likely to be hailed by a watchman and urged to stop for dinner. Often guests stayed for days or weeks or months. It was in this way that the plantations gained a reputation for extravagant hospitality, and also acquired the debts that were constantly threatening to topple them to ruin.

Three sugar cones and a tub of tea decorate this merchant's sign.

Boot and shoemaker's sign.
(Colonial Williamsburg)

Sociability was also provided by the weekly churchgoing. For the Virginians, religion was never the heavy burden it was for the Puritans in the North. The Virginia planters had not come to the new land to worship God in freedom; they had come to gain wealth and ease. They were loyal to the Church of England, and most families attended church regularly. But they did not trouble themselves about the sin and salvation that tormented the Puritans, and they did not believe that it was sinful to enjoy themselves. Philip Fithian, the young tutor who wrote about the ladies' head coverings, had studied at Princeton for the ministry, and he was scandalized at the casual observance of the Sabbath that he found in his new home. He once wrote:

> A Sunday in Virginia don't seem to wear the same dress as our Sundays to the northward . . . All the lower class of people, and the servants, and the slaves, consider it as a day of pleasure and amusement . . . The gentlemen go to church, to be sure, but they make that itself a matter of convenience, and account the church a useful weekly resort to do business.

Colonial Williamsburg

The trip which Byrd and his wife quarreled about was the greatest social event of the year. William Byrd was a representative from his county to the House of Burgesses which met twice a year for a two-week period filled with the gayest of social whirls. He must have known that, plucked eyebrows or no, nothing could have induced Madam Byrd to stay at home.

The House of Burgesses is outstanding in the history of America as the first example of representative government in the colonies. In this famous assembly the first protests were made against taxation without representation, the stirring speeches of Patrick Henry and Thomas Jefferson roused the people to rebellion, and the Declaration of Independence had its origin.

At the time of William Byrd, however, the assembly was less a political affair than an occasion for a gathering of the whole countryside. Williamsburg had lately been made the capital of Virginia, and there the royal governor resided in a handsome palace. In the spring and fall, when the legislature convened, every inn and dwelling house in this normally quiet town was filled to overflowing. Planters and their families moved into their town houses. The days were filled with military parades, horse races, and fashionable dinners, balls and theater parties. From the account in Byrd's diary, we can guess that Madam Byrd soon forgot her complaints.

> *About seven o'clock the company went in coaches from the Governor's house to the capitol where the Governor opened the ball with a French dance with my wife ... Then we danced country dances for an hour and the company was carried into another room where was a very fine collation of sweetmeats. The Governor was very gallant to the ladies and very courteous to the gentlemen. About 2 o'clock the company returned to their coaches and because the drive was dirty the Governor carried the ladies into their coaches.*

A wigmaker's sign and a blacksmith's trade card. (Colonial Williamsburg)

Not only the wealthy enjoyed these public times. Virginians of all ranks flocked to the inns and coffeehouses of Williamsburg. In the crowded days of sports and races, tavern dances and drinking bouts, they did not envy in the least an invitation to the governor's ball. In addition, twice a year, in April and December, a great fair was held in Market Square in front of the courthouse. Here the farmers exchanged their livestock, held auctions, and reveled in cockfights, puppet shows, cudgeling bouts, country dances and fiddling contests.

Today we can see Williamsburg almost as it was at the time of Byrd's visit there. The Governor's Palace, the beautiful brick mansions, the inns and rows of shops have been rebuilt and refurnished, so that the tourist steps back into the eighteenth century with all its charm and grace—though the powder house and the jail with its leg-irons and pillory remind us that life there was not always happy and serene.

Though we have chosen to describe the life of Virginia, other Southern colonies, such as South Carolina and Maryland, have stories equally worth telling. Charles Town, in South Carolina, where the wealth of the plantations depended not on tobacco but on rice and indigo, was at the time of the Revolution the third most important seaport in the colonies. It was a city so luxurious and beautiful that John Quincy wrote that it surpassed all he ever saw, or ever expected to see, in America. For the privileged class at least, Captain John Smith's prophecy of Virginia had come true. They would have said with him that "heaven and earth never agreed better to frame a place for man's habitation."

MEREDITH JUMP,

*U*NTIL lately HAMMERMAN of *Lightfoot*, has taken the SMITH'S SHOP & FORGE formerly conducted by *Elkanah Deane*, at the HORSE HEAD, in *Prince George* Street, near the Church at WILLIAMSBURG, where he carries on the Smith's Trade in all its Branches. He makes a great Variety of ORNAMENTAL & USEFUL IRON ARTICLES, which are sold through his Agents otherwise, and will welcome all Such as care to inspect his Premises.

New England Neighbors

2

In their little villages New Englanders led a very different life from that of the Southern colonists. Most New Englanders were farmers, but unlike the sprawling plantations of the south their farms were clustered in friendly settlements. Often a group of church members in a town would plan to break away and establish their own church and village. As soon as they had chosen the new site, they portioned out tidy farm lots, side by side. Working together, they built their houses reassuringly in sight of one another for neighborliness, for protection, and for common worship. Behind each house a few acres of farmland stretched back.

Usually the houses were set in two rows, separated by a wide band of open field known as the green or common, where all the cows and sheep in the village grazed together. Later on, land outside the village was set aside as a pasture, and the green became the center of community life. Here, prominently in view, were the pillory, the stocks and the whipping post. Here the village militia lined up for parade and inspection. Neighbors paused to greet each other and to chat. Today a welcoming, tree-shaded green is still to be found in most New England towns.

The New England village was a little world in itself. Yet each one grew in much the same pattern—one which had its beginning in the first settlement at Plymouth.

Experiment in Neighborliness

In the first difficult year at Plymouth in 1621 the Pilgrims tried to share all the land in common and to work together for the general welfare. The *Mayflower* passengers had a heavy debt to repay to the company in London which had financed their voyage. And they knew from their first discouraging glimpse of the bleak shore of New England that only by co-operation and self-sacrifice could they survive. During that first winter a terrible sickness took the lives of half their number, till only fifty remained. As one after another fell ill, the loyalty of every member was tested to the utmost. William Bradford, their governor, tells us in his account that:

> *in the time of most distress, there was but six or seven sound persons . . . who spared no pains night nor day, but with abundance of toil and hazard of their own health, fetched them wood, made them fires, dressed them meat, made their beds, washed their loathsome clothes, clothed and unclothed them . . . and all this willingly and cheerfully, without any grudging in the least . . .*

While their families waited on the Mayflower, the men built a common house on shore.

The first Boston Town House, built
in 1658, had a market place on the
ground floor, meeting rooms above.

In the second year the experiment in common property came to an end. The Pilgrims were forced to admit that it had not been a success. The hard workers objected to laboring over cornfields in which the lazy members would have equal share. So lots were portioned out to each family, and men worked twice as hard, knowing that their own families would reap the crops they sowed. With the second harvest the Pilgrims enjoyed true plenty, and never again did Plymouth endure a famine.

Soon after the founding of Plymouth other bands of Puritans set sail for America. The first group settled on the coast of Massachusetts at Salem. Another group established the Massachusetts Bay Colony near Boston. These Puritans were for the most part well-to-do businessmen, farmers and tradesmen. They brought with them the supplies which the Pilgrims had lacked—tools, clothing, food and livestock. Although they knew hardship, they never had to endure a starving time such as Plymouth had known. From the beginning they were able to build better houses, and to set up a prosperous trade with England.

Gradually settlements spread across Massachusetts and Rhode Island and Connecticut and north into New Hampshire and Maine and Vermont. When we speak of the "frontier" we sometimes think of the mountain regions of Ohio and Kentucky and of the Western plains. There was always an American frontier, and in the beginning it was in New England, only a few miles from the Atlantic coast. As the colonists pushed ever farther to the west, each new settlement repeated in its own way the story of Jamestown and Plymouth. Striking out into the wilderness, each small group had to clear a place in the forest and build their first cabins with their own hands.

Settlers often found their first shelters in caves and holes. Edward Johnson, an early historian, wrote of them:

> *They burrow themselves in the earth . . . under some hill-side, casting the earth aloft upon timber; they make a smoky fire against the earth at the highest side . . . keeping off the showers from their lodgings, but long rains penetrate through . . .*

Damp and crowded and smoky, these little holes often sheltered whole families for months or even years till a house could be built. In some settlements families built wigwams of branches. We can judge the enormous labor of building a house from the fact that after a year at Plymouth only seven houses had been built, and Governor Bradford wrote that "many of our arms and legs can tell us to this day" of the labor. To build a house a man had first to clear the land, to fell the great trees and square the rough logs with his broadax. He had to dig the square trench that would mark the dimensions of his house, and wrest from the frozen soil the stones that would form its foundation. Then he could begin to set the first heavy corner posts.

A bed wrench, used to tighten the ropes of rope-slung beds.
(Old Sturbridge Village)

A trundle bed (so called because it was trundled under a big bed) being heated with a warming pan.

New England Puritans did not build true log cabins. Like the Jamestown settlers, they tried to make their houses as much as possible like the ones they had left behind in England. Their first dwellings were low, one-room houses much like the Southern houses, except that the chimneys were built into the corners to conserve the warmth. They also used oiled paper for their windows, but there is an interesting record in New Hampshire of windows made of woodchuck skin, the hair removed, the skin rubbed thin, well greased, and stretched over a frame.

Such a cabin was so cramped that a family hardly minded the scarcity of furniture. One thing every Northern family wanted was a settle for the fireplace, a narrow bench with a very high back to shut out the drafts. Often a built-in platform in one corner served for a bed, with a fat mattress stuffed with feathers or straw. Pushed under the platform was a small trundle bed, which was pulled out for the children at night. The handmade cradle was close to the hearth, or near the spinning wheel, where an occasional prod from the spinner's foot could set the wooden rockers in motion.

In the depths of the hearth a fire was kept always burning, summer or winter, not only for cooking but because once it went out it had to be started with flint and steel. A quicker way was to send a child running to the nearest neighbor to borrow a shovelful of hot coals. The fire also gave light to the gloomy room.

At night the settlers lighted pine-knots, which contained a pitch that burned with a clear light. This "candle-wood" gave off a thick smoke and dropped bits of melted pitch, so the knots were practical only when stuck in the stones of the fireplace. Every precious bit of fat from game or mutton was saved to make torches of rushes soaked in grease or to burn in "betty lamps," which were small iron saucers hung on chains. Later,

A fire-carrier used to bring hot coals from a neighbor's hearth. (New-York Historical Society)

29

when fat was more plentiful, the colonists had the luxury of tallow candles.

As the years went by, and life in the settlements became a little easier, a man could make improvements on his first cabin. Perhaps he nailed clapboards, first called clayboards, on the outside to keep out the cold, and plastered a rough daubing of clay on the walls within. He might add a room for sleeping on the other side of the chimney, or a little lean-to behind the house. When he built a new house it would have a second story for the sleeping rooms. His new roof would be shingled instead of thatched, and it was likely to be gabled to make small attic chambers, or to be broken by one or two small dormer windows. He might be able to afford panes of glass for his casement windows. He would surely have a wooden floor which his wife would keep well scrubbed and covered with a layer of fine white sand swirled in fancy patterns with a turkey feather.

He could be very proud of the furniture in his new house. By the end of the seventeenth century cabinetmakers in New England were making furniture as handsome as any that could be imported from England. There would be a fine carved chest for the family linen, chairs and tables with turned legs, four-poster beds, even small, rather cloudy mirrors. There might be a carpet, not on the floor but as a table covering.

The heart of every house was the kitchen, with its huge fireplace which could burn logs six feet long. Ranged about the hearth were the iron kettles and skillets, the long forks and tongs, the bellows to blow up the fire, and the warming pan, which would be filled with hot coals and carried upstairs at night to be thrust between icy sheets. The wide, high-backed settle still sat cozily near by. On narrow shelves along the wall were the wooden dishes and noggins which served the family at meals, and the pewter plates and mugs which were the family pride.

The Puritan Sabbath

One good way to understand the Puritans is to watch them on the Sabbath Day. No matter how bitter a struggle it was just to keep alive, the Puritans held first in their minds their duty to God. They were convinced that they had been chosen by God for a special purpose and that they must live every moment in a God-fearing manner. They fiercely resented the slightest difference in belief. Although they had left England to escape intolerance, they had no intention of allowing freedom of worship in the new colony. The one exception was Roger Williams' settlement in Rhode Island, where he offered a haven even to Quakers, who in Massachusetts were branded and whipped and even hanged.

The difficulty was that not all the colonists were Puritans. On every ship that sailed for America, even the *Mayflower,* there were poor men who wanted only an opportunity to make a decent living for their families in the New World. These men were loyal to the Church of England, and they found it hard to understand or share the zeal of the Puritans. But the powerful religious leaders made the laws. Every man, woman and child, member or no, attended meeting on the Sabbath without question. When they lapsed from grace they were punished by heavy fines, or by the

Pounding grain in a mortar mill was made easier by the springiness of a young sapling.

*A New Bedford,
Massachusetts, street scene
about 1800. (New York
Public Library)*

stocks and the whipping post. Moreover, Puritan rules dominated every day of the week.

Let us look in on a meeting house on the Sabbath. It might be a meeting in Plymouth, Boston, or another early town, for country folk everywhere in New England were to follow very much the same pattern for more than a hundred years. Preparations for the Sabbath began the day before, when all food had to be cooked and clothes made ready. No labor, not even a last-minute stitch, could be done on the Sabbath. As in ancient Hebrew law, the Sabbath began at sundown the night before, and the evening was spent in prayer and Bible reading. In the morning the roll of a drum sounded across the fields. Sometimes a horn or a conch shell, or even a gun, summoned the worshipers, for the early meeting houses had no bells in their small turrets. Clapboard Hill in Fairfield, Connecticut, is said to have been so named because the parish there was summoned to meeting by beating two clapboards together. At the second summons the townsfolk came soberly from their houses.

Inside the small bare building they took their proper places, men on one side, women on the other. The deacons sat at the front, just below the pulpit. The correct seating in churches was a ticklish matter. Everyone agreed "the first pew to be the highest in dignity," and the precise order of the choice places caused bitter feuds. One town in Connecticut settled the argument by giving the best seats to those who had paid the most toward the church building. Servants and slaves crowded near the door or climbed

to a loft or balcony. Boys did not sit with their parents but were crowded
together in one spot, perhaps the stairs to the balcony, where they were
expected to sit in complete silence through the long service.

The service began with a prayer by the minister. A good prayer lasted
for at least an hour, after which the people rose, very thankfully, no
doubt, for the psalm. Puritans, in their anxiety to avoid any suggestion of
the Church of England, frowned especially on music. For hymn singing
they substituted a "lining of the psalm." A deacon read one line at a time,
setting the tune by memory, and the congregation droned each line after
him. It was many years before any musical instrument was allowed. When
a wealthy Boston gentleman once willed to his church his own pipe organ,
imported from England, the members voted to refuse it.

After the psalm came the sermon. An inspired minister could preach
for two, three, even four hours, and the hearts of his youngest listeners
must have sunk each time he turned over the hourglass that stood on the
pulpit. Their parents listened intently to the terrible warnings of sin and
punishment. But they were hard-working people, and even on the wooden
benches they sometimes began to nod. Ladies sniffed sprigs of fennel to

ward off sleepiness. Shameful as it was to be caught dozing in meetings, the elders never trusted their congregations. They provided a "tithingman" to keep watch, armed with a long pole, at one end of which was a feather or a squirrel's tail, at the other a round knob. The ladies needed only a tickling reminder, but in the town records of Stratford, Connecticut, we find the following order:

> It was agreed that Henry Wakelee shall watch over the youths or any disorderly carriages in the time of public worship on the Lord's day or other time and see that they behave themselves comely and note any disorderly persons by such raps or blows as he in his discretion shall see meet.

Churches were unheated, and for many months of the year must have been unbearably cold. Judge Sewall of Boston recorded in his famous diary one Sunday, "This day so cold that the sacramental bread is frozen pretty hard, and rattles sadly as broken in the plates." Often the ice had to be broken in the christening bowl before a poor shivering infant could be baptized. Women carried with them from home small footstoves full of hot coals on which to rest their thin slippers, but the heat dwindled long before the sermon. Undoubtedly the minister had the best of it—he could wave his arms to emphasize his threats of doom!

At noontime those who lived near by returned to their warm firesides. Others, who had come from a distance on foot or horseback, spent the noon hour in long sheds or in little Sabbath houses especially built for this purpose. There they could light a fire and heat their meager lunches of beans or cornbread and thaw out their fingers and toes before returning for the afternoon service, which was just as long as the morning one. When the long day was ended they went home to spend the evening discussing the sermons.

Strict rules regulated every aspect of the Sabbath. In every colony there were long lists of fines for Sabbath-breaking—three shillings for young folks who played at meeting, forty shillings for singing, running or jumping. Since two shillings was a good day's pay, it was prudent to obey the rules. But in spite of all the discomforts, the Puritans really enjoyed their Sabbath. There were few other occasions when they could wear their best clothes, or rest their weary muscles, or enjoy a talk with their neighbors. And the sermon, with all its terrors, gave them something to think about for the whole week to come.

The Witchcraft Fever

There was one grim aspect of Puritan life that seems almost unbelievable to us today. That was the fanatical belief in witches. The Puritans did not invent this belief. The world of that day was filled with superstition and fear, and in Europe and England thousands of innocent men and women

In an age of three-hour sermons, the preacher made much use of his hourglass, and the tithingman tickled a drowsy listener with a feather-tipped stick.

Hot coals placed in this stove warmed a woman's freezing feet during meeting. (Old Sturbridge Village)

had been convicted of witchcraft and put to death. For the Puritans, witchcraft seemed entirely believable, because they were certain that the Devil was ever-present, stalking about the world to work evil. They believed that men and women could sell themselves to the Devil and receive from him the power to do all sorts of mysterious mischief. Ignorance strengthened this belief. So little was known about science and medicine that a sudden attack of pain, or an epidemic that raged through a village, or any unusual misfortune could only be explained by some evil influence. In such cases the blame was fastened on any person who had aroused suspicion or dislike by being different from his neighbors. Women were most often suspected. A witch might be a solitary old woman who mumbled to herself or to her cat, or who had a sharp tongue and a dislike for little boys in her vegetable patch. Or she might be a pretty young woman who was overbold or impudent. It was easy to believe that anyone who was odd was "in league with Satan" and it took very slight evidence to prove it in court.

A child woke screaming from a nightmare and insisted that a black furry creature sat at the foot of his bed. His terrified parents were sure that old Goody Brown had taken this shape to torment their child. Goodman Brown went out into the field of an evening to call in his cows and found them unable to move a step. Looking up, he saw a young girl standing by the field, and when she moved away, the cows came as willingly as ever to be milked. A fastidious woman who said that she scorned "to be drabbled" with dirt managed to walk over a muddy road without being spattered, proving that she had surely been carried by the Devil, and she paid for her neatness by being hanged. These are true cases. On such ridiculous evidence witches were convicted in the courts of New England. Ministers, the best-educated and respected men of the day, took part in such witch trials, and even quoted Bible passages to justify the death penalty.

The hunt for witches reached a terrible climax in Salem, Massachusetts, in 1693, when panic and hatred seemed to take possession of the whole town. Mainly on the testimony of a few screaming hysterical children, nineteen witches were put to death. This frenzy shocked all New England, and people began to come to their senses. Years later, Judge Sewall, who had helped to pass sentence on these innocent people, realized the sin he had committed and humbled himself to confess it in meeting, too late, of course, to help the ones he had wronged or their grieving families. Very soon colonial courts refused to convict anyone of witchcraft, but for a long time ignorant and superstitious people continued to whisper about broomsticks and spells.

The Lighter Side

Puritan life has been made to sound exceedingly grim. But we wonder. Why were so many rules and regulations needed if the Puritans were

40   COBWEBS TO CATCH FLIES.

THE COTTAGE GARDEN.

FIRST BOY.

I see no toys—How do you pass your time?*

SECOND BOY.

I feed the hens, and the ducks; I see the calf fed.

FIRST BOY.

And what do you do else?

SECOND BOY.

I go out and see the men plough; I see them sow ; and when I am good, they give me some corn.

FIRST BOY.

And what do you do with it ?

A page from a primer of the 1830's. (New York Public Library)

A gossip, or scold, strapped to a ducking stool gets a drenching in the town pond.

always stern and sober? Just a glimpse at the fines imposed in any town meeting shows us that the Puritans were certainly human. And we are misled by pictures which show them always dressed in black and gray. The Puritans did dress plainly; their ministers railed against anything luxurious or showy. We are all familiar with the Puritan in black doublet, baggy breeches, simple white linen collar, plain, wide-brimmed hat and square-cut serviceable shoes. We picture his wife in simple, long-sleeved dress and petticoats of homespun, with neckerchief, cuffs and apron of white linen, and the kerchief or hood that modestly covered her head whenever she stepped from her own doorway. But the Puritans liked colors. The women dyed their homespun garments in soft blues, and in the browns and dull greens and purples they called "sad" colors. The men of the Massachusetts Bay Company wore green cotton waistcoats and red knit caps. And even Elder Brewster of Plymouth had a violet coat!

Frothy ruffles, sleeves slit to reveal brilliant linings, high boots trimmed with silk rosettes and buckles—all these things were forbidden. Since the Cavaliers of England sported rows of buttons just for decoration, the Puritans scorned to use buttons even to hold their jackets together, and they went to all sorts of trouble to devise loops and ties and "points." Silk in any form was frowned upon, since it was both costly and perishable. In fact, what the Puritan leaders most deplored was any attempt to dress beyond one's income. A woman who wore a silk gown often had to prove in court that her husband could afford it.

Fashion is hard to subdue. Our forefathers were prepared to make many sacrifices, but they would not give up their small vanities. A sprinkling of bows and buttons, gilt braid and lace constantly distracted

35

the attention of worshipers on the Sabbath. One young woman who was reproved for wearing a bow on her bonnet appeared the following Sabbath with two bows! As soon as the hardships of the early days were forgotten, the Puritans forgot their scruples. A man might add silver buckles to his shoes, or embroidered sleeves to his waistcoat. His wife would order a scarlet cloak or a silk gown from London. The church fathers fought a losing battle. By 1700 their once-sober members flaunted every kind of extravagance.

Although early New Englanders looked with suspicion on any pleasure that could be considered worldly or frivolous, they wholeheartedly enjoyed the few entertainments they allowed themselves. They had their Training Day and Thursday lectures by the minister, and they relished a funeral, where they partook of food and drink and received a souvenir in the form of a funeral ring or scarf or a pair of gloves. Public punishments on the village green always drew a crowd, and the greatest show of all was a public execution, complete with a long sermon by the minister and a solemn speech of repentance and warning by the condemned man.

There were also house-raisings and stone-haulings and corn-huskings and apple-paring parties, where the hard work that had to be done anyway was turned into an occasion for laughter and gossip and a feast of cakes and pies with ample rounds of cider and rum. The Puritans were hearty eaters and even more hearty drinkers. Boys and men hunted and fished together, and girls and women gossiped happily over their spinning.

And romance flourished, even in that first dreadful year at Plymouth, when John Alden courted Priscilla Mullens. Since the Sabbath officially ended at sundown, Sunday evening was a favorite time for young men to go courting. A man had to take his courage with him, for in most homes the kitchen was the only warm room in the house, and the romance had to be conducted from opposite sides of the fireplace, in the presence of father and mother and inquisitive relatives and giggling younger brothers and sisters. Some parents, remembering the days when they too had longed to speak for each other's ears alone, allowed the young people to whisper through a long hollow rod.

In a day when the strictest rules governed everyone's behavior, and when unchaperoned dating was unheard of, it is odd that the custom of bundling was quite common, at least in the rural sections of New England. When the old folks went to bed in the corner, the fire died down and the kitchen grew too cold for entertaining. If a young man lived too far to ride home, he "tarried," and the couple bundled up, fully dressed, in a bed, where, still chaperoned, they could whisper cozily till morning.

We may not envy the lives of the Puritans, but we can be proud of them. Though they seem to us stern and joyless, there is no doubt that without their fortitude and self-sacrifice they would have failed in this harsh wilderness.

Lacking a mill, two men saw their own planks.

After helping with a house-raising, the neighbors could always look forward to feasting.

A contemporary engraving showing the turbulence that sometimes took over at a town meeting of the 1790's. (Library of Congress)

TOWN MEETING.

Cradle of Democracy

Before the Pilgrims went ashore at Plymouth they held a solemn meeting and signed an agreement which has come down in history as the May-flower Compact. They bound themselves to "combine ourselves together into a Civil Body Politic, for our better ordering and preservation" and "to enact . . . such just and equal laws . . . as shall be thought most meet and convenient for the general good of the Colony."

This agreement was a temporary and practical measure. The Pilgrims knew that here in the wilderness they must maintain their own law and order. They did not realize that in the Mayflower Compact they were taking a tremendous step toward independence, not only in choosing their own governor, a thing which no English colony had ever done before, but simply in meeting together as equals to decide what was best for them all. Every New England settlement thereafter followed their example, the leading men meeting together to settle important questions by vote. As years went by, this custom resulted in the town meeting, a method of popular government which has continued in American towns to this day.

Of course, for many years the New England town meetings were not really democratic. Women, who had no right to an opinion anyway, and servants and workingmen who owned no property were excluded. And in the beginning such meetings were actually church meetings. To have a vote a man had to be not only a landowner but a church member in good standing. This tight control by the church was loosened only very slowly. By the end of the seventeenth century voters were no longer required to be church members, but everywhere in the colonies they had to be property holders. Though land was plentiful and cheap, still large numbers

A pumpkin shell was used as a guide in giving country boys the short haircut required by Connecticut Blue Laws. (New York Public Library)

of artisans and workers, servants and slaves were disqualified. In Massachusetts, even at the time of George Washington's election, only one man in sixteen was eligible to vote.

At a town meeting every detail of community life was debated and decided by vote, from the salary of the new schoolmaster to the men who would represent the town in the colonial assembly. Ancient records of town meetings, in faded handwriting and astonishing spelling, give us a vivid picture of village life.

The same problems seem to have vexed the taxpayers in every town. There were always complaints of careless townsfolk who let their swine wander into their neighbors' cornfields, who forgot to close the common pasture gates, who neglected to keep up their fences, and let briars and weeds grow across the road. There were constant petty lawsuits about livestock that had not been branded. In Andover, New Hampshire, paupers were "struck off" or boarded out to the lowest bidders. Then there was the troublesome matter of strangers, for every town guarded its membership carefully and suspected all outsiders. In most towns any person who entertained a stranger, even a relative, had to report his guest to the town authorities. Desirable newcomers were "voted in," but undesirables were "warned out" and asked to leave town. Greenwich, Connecticut, passed a law in 1665 stating that "none shall be admitted to be an inhabitant but only such who shall bring . . . a certificate to testifie of their orderly life and conversation . . ." Even after the Revolution strangers were still warned out of New England towns. Arguments in town meeting were also sure to arise between ambitious folk with ideas about a bell for the steeple or a new schoolhouse and thrifty folk who objected to spending the money. Town meetings were surely never dull. No detail seems to have been too small to receive the town's attention. In one town in 1649 three women were fined for scolding, and in another town a man was fined for winning the affections of a girl without first getting her parents' consent.

At these meetings the town officers were elected, usually for a term of one year. A young and inexperienced householder might start at the bottom of the ladder as a Fence Viewer, making sure that the pasture fences were kept in good repair. Or he might be elected a Scaler of Weights and Measures, to inspect the scales and see that no farmer was cheating his customers. He could look forward to the dignity of someday serving as Town Clerk or even as one of the Selectmen. At one time or another he would probably have to take his turn at the unpopular job of Constable. He might serve as the Tithingman, who kept order on the Sabbath, the Surveyor of Highways, the Sheepmaster, the Cowkeeper, the Overseer of the Poor, the Drummer or the Town Crier, the Digger of Graves, the Sweeper of the Meeting House, or the Ringer of the Bell. Or he might serve as Poundkeeper, holding stray animals in a little stone-walled pound till their owners paid a fine to redeem them.

Though these early town meetings were not entirely democratic, they provided an excellent training ground for the citizens of a future democracy. Thomas Jefferson once said of them, "They have proved themselves

A view of Connecticut state prison showing the inmates being marched from the workshop to the guardhouse while (at right) a guard flogs a prisoner. (Connecticut Historical Society)

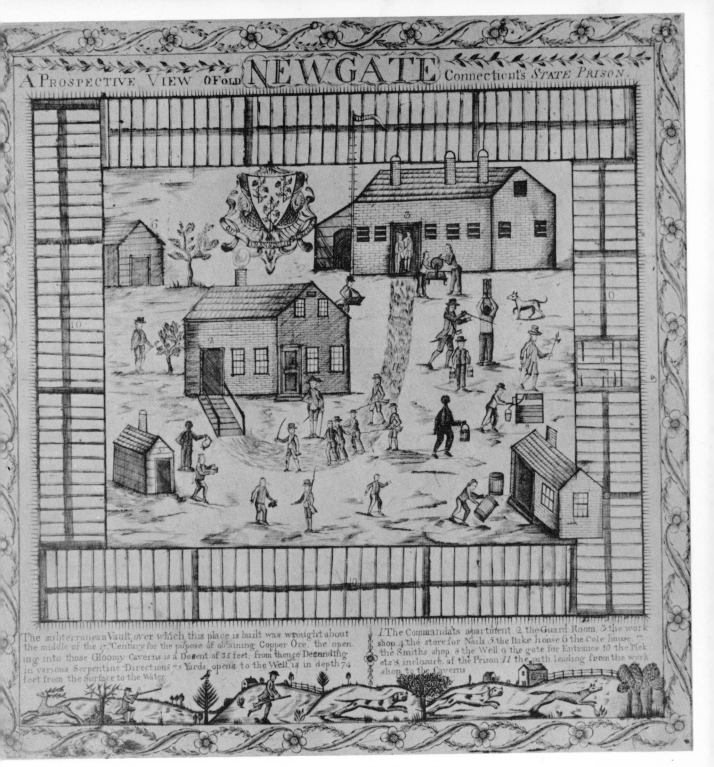

A PROSPECTIVE VIEW OF OLD NEWGATE Connecticut's STATE PRISON.

The subterranean Vault over which this place is built was wrought about the middle of the 17.ᵗʰ Century for the purpose of obtaining Copper Ore, the opening into those Gloomy Caverns is a Descent of 35 feet; from thence Descending in various Serpentine Directions 75 Yards, opens to the Well is in depth 74 feet from the Surface to the Water.

1 The Commandats apartment 2 the Guard Room 3 the work shop 4 the store for Nails 5 the Bake house 6 the Cole house 7 the Smiths shop 8 the Well 9 the gate for Entrance 10 the Picketts's inclosure of the Prison 11 the path leading from the work shop to the Caverns

the wisest invention ever devised by the wit of man for the perfect exercise of self-government and for its preservation."

Village Folk

By the mid-eighteenth century, hundreds of snug little villages and towns dotted the New England countryside, similar in appearance, in their pattern of growth, their manner of thinking, and their unique and independent life. The neighborliness which began in the Plymouth colony had grown into the American way of life. Edward Johnson, who wrote about the early cabins, commented, "The Lord hath been pleased to turn all the wigwams, huts and hovels the English dwelt in at their first coming, into orderly, fair, and well-built houses well-furnished, many of them, together with orchards filled with goodly fruit trees, and gardens with variety of flowers."

In the New England village each man lived with his family, free and self-reliant, on his own small farm. Yet he was dependent on his neighbors. In time of trouble or sickness, or for a task too big for his hands alone, he could rely on their willing help. When he built a new barn or married off a daughter, he invited them to celebrate with him. Everyone minded everyone else's business. Neighbors might quarrel, but in an emergency they all banded loyally together. At one time, in Northampton, Massachusetts, when a man lost his shop by fire, every other shop in town closed its doors, the shopkeepers turned out with axes and hammers, and within a week had built a new shop and set him up in business again.

The New England farmer raised almost everything needed by the family. In his fields he planted corn and rye, perhaps oats, barley or wheat. In his vegetable garden there flourished potatoes, pumpkins, onions, peas, beans, squash and cabbages. In his orchard stood rows of sturdy apple, peach and pear trees. He might have a small field of flax. In his stable he had the necessary ox or two, but only rarely a horse to ride. In the pastureland behind his fields there grazed a few cows, and sheep, and a hog or two fattened for the winter supply of salt pork. A flock of chickens and a family of geese or ducks pecked in the dirt in front of the barn.

In her spacious, comfortable kitchen, his wife made thrifty use of all these products. Every fruit and vegetable that could be dried or preserved or pickled was laid away for the winter months. Butter was churned and

Above: A cradle scythe for harvesting grain.

Right: Hand-carved wooden grain shovel.

(Old Sturbridge Village)

cheese pressed into great wheels. And whatever the family could spare was sent to the city as barter for the few necessities the land did not provide—sugar and salt, molasses, spices, tea and coffee.

Flax from the field was made into linen for the beds, napkins for the table, and curtains for the windows. Wool from the sheep was spun and woven into practical shirts and jackets and dresses, and knit into thick warm stockings. On winter evenings the farmer made leather shoes for his whole family. Many a country boy never wore a store-bought article of clothing till he became a man. Then, if he bought for his wedding a good Sabbath suit, a beaver hat, and a pair of boots, he expected these things to last a lifetime. Not for him were the silks and satins and powdered wigs of the city gentleman. For hard work in the fields, leather breeches served him well enough. His wife was perhaps more aware of the distant world of fashion. Her homemade petticoats might balloon over a modest hoop, and her clever fingers might fashion a calash or bonnet like one she had seen on a visit to town. Country girls learned to plait the long grasses into copies of the stylish straw hats their city cousins ordered from Europe. A bride might even cherish a string of gold beads. But she seldom owned more than one good dress at a time. Country people had an honest scorn for city trappings. There is a story told of a lady in Windsor, Connecticut, whose husband brought her from the West Indies the latest novelty—an oiled linen umbrella with rattan sticks. When she dared to appear with it, her neighbors made fun of her by walking about with sieves tied atop broom handles.

Farmers in the villages still lived in simple, four-room houses like those their Puritan grandparents had built, some weathered to a soft gray, some painted red. It was a time of large families, and extra rooms might be added. The popular "salt-box" house had a long sloping roof in the rear to cover extra one-story rooms.

White Houses on the Green

The homes of the leading townsfolk, which faced the green, showed how rapidly both the prosperity and the tastes of the colonists had grown. Most architects agree that no other houses built in America equal in beauty and dignity these houses of the last half of the eighteenth century, houses still comfortable to live in today. Their fine proportions, their graceful doorways, their handsomely paneled, high-ceilinged rooms all reflect a gracious and cultured way of life.

The rich furnishings of these houses were evidence not only of the

Right: Wooden pitchfork.

Below: Early New England plow.

(Old Sturbridge Village)

growing wealth of the colonies but also of the trade which now reached to every corner of the world. There were French wallpapers, rugs from the Orient, Chinese porcelain cups, thin as eggshells, and woven coverlets from India. But most of the furniture bore the stamp of American craftsmen. Just as the plain sturdy furniture of the Pilgrims reflected their spare hard way of life, the light and delicate furniture of the eighteenth century indicated more leisurely and prosperous times. Silversmiths were fashioning lovely and intricately-decorated pieces—teapots and bowls and candlesticks. Paul Revere's mark was on many of the finest.

But, surprisingly, the kitchens of these fine houses differed very little from those of the small red farmhouses. Though the food was now ele-

The country store was a place for gossip and checker-playing as well as a source of everything from cheese to bird cages. Facing page: An iron auger used to loosen brown sugar stored in barrels, and, below, a lantern of the Paul Revere type. (New-York Historical Society)

gantly served in a paneled dining room, the methods of cooking it had not changed. There was the ancient crane and the array of iron kettles, the brick oven for bread-making, the crude iron forks and tongs. Certainly the leisurely way of life had not penetrated the kitchen. But we suspect that the ladies of the house, with their hoopskirts and embroidery frames, were not greatly concerned with the convenience of the kitchen. There were servants to lift the heavy kettles and to bake the bread. We can still see in the attics of some of these houses the slave quarters, built high under the eaves, close to the chimney to catch any escaping warmth, appallingly dismal and cramped in contrast to the spacious beauty of the rooms below.

The Steeple Bell

Still dominating the village green, and indeed the whole village, was the meeting house. The first boxlike structure with its squat little turret had been replaced now by a graceful white-painted building with a slender spire lifted against the sky. Usually this was the Congregational Church which had evolved from the Puritan meeting house, but now a church, such as the Episcopal or Presbyterian, shared the green, for New England had somewhat outgrown its early intolerance. Religion was still of the utmost importance for these people, but it was no longer the heavy burden it had been for their Puritan grandparents. There were still two services every Sunday, but three-hour sermons were rare, the tithingman was disappearing, the service was enlivened by hymn-singing, and occasionally a mother even brought sugarplums to bribe the youngest into sitting quietly.

Not only on the Sabbath but every day in the week the bell in the steeple guided the townsfolk through their daily lives. At noontime it called the farmers from the fields for dinner. Sometimes a series of quick strokes announced the day of the month. The nine o'clock bell marked the end of the day, a signal for guests to depart and for couples loitering on the green to say good night. The passing bell made everyone in the village at once aware of a death. People would pause in their work to count. Nine strokes for a man, six for a woman, three for a child, followed by short strokes which gave the age of the one who had died. Later the townsfolk would follow the coffin to the small cemetery to the accompaniment of a steady tolling. But the bell could also jangle in celebration. News of the British surrender at Yorktown spread across the country to the pealing of bells.

Country Stores, Cobblers and Blacksmiths

At first the only tradesmen in the village had been wandering peddlers, with pack on back, tempting the country housewives with indigo and spices and scissors and combs. Sooner or later one of these was certain to settle down and open a store.

The New England country store was a hodgepodge of spicy smells, candy jars, cracker barrels, and a medley of everything from needles and pins and beaver hats to pitchforks and horsewhips. It was crowded and dimly lighted, with no wall space spared for windows. A good idea of the items on display can be gained from an advertisement that appeared in a newspaper in Danbury, Connecticut, in 1790:

NICHOLS AND DIBBLE

Have just received at their store at Great Plain and are now selling exceeding cheap for ready pay the following articles:
Blue, bottle-green, London smoke, scarlet and mix't broadcloth. Coatings, frizes, velvets, satinets, chintzes, calicoes, wild-boars, camblers, calimanco, stuffs, baizes, flannels, shalloons, muslin, gauze, silk handkerchiefs, cotton do, shawls, worsted hose, modes, sarcenets, laces, ribbons, ostrich feathers, silk and twist, coat and vest buttons. A complete assortment of hardware and crockery, rum, wine, Geneva, brown sugar, loaf sugar, lump sugar, tea, chocolate, raisins, allspice, pepper, indigo, snuff, alum, copperas, soap, redwood, dogwood, Spanish brown, 6 × 8 glass, German steel, etc.
All kinds of country produce will be received in payment, and every favor gratefully acknowledged. Good rock salt exchanged for flax seed, or rye, even.

The village store might even boast one of the little cast-iron stoves manufactured by the Germans in Pennsylvania. This would be a magnet for chilly customers who liked to linger for a discussion about crops or politics. In summer they would gather about the little open porch in front. The general store was a friendly, leisurely place. The storekeeper, who was usually the postmaster as well, knew the habits and peculiarities of everyone in town and was an expert at juggling the intricate system of barter that served most country folk in place of cash.

In a prosperous village there would be one or two other shops as well. One of these might be a cobbler's shop. Shoes ordered from a cobbler would seem a shocking luxury to a farmer who had always made shoes for his family. But since they would likely be worn only for meeting on the Sabbath and during the coldest weather, they were guaranteed to last for a long time. It was quite common for a country family to walk to church barefoot, carrying their shoes with them, and to put them on outside the door of the meeting house. Sometimes the housewife wore an old pair which she hid in the bushes before reaching the church.

A child's first visit to the cobbler's shop must have been an adventure. How important he must have felt as he placed his foot firmly on the leather and watched the cobbler trace an outline around it. How curiously he must have stared about at the rows of lasts hanging on the wall—only one to a size or customer, because the shoes would be identical, right and left, and could be changed about. He would watch the

A wooden pestle was used to pound grain in this mortar.
(Old Sturbridge Village)

An early gristmill, powered by the water wheel at left, ground grain into meal between two large millstones.

cobbler as, hunched over his bench, he bored holes in the leather with his awl and sewed soles and uppers together with a needle made from a hog's bristle and thread stiffened with beeswax. Waiting on a shelf there might be a delicate pair of silk and brocade slippers ordered by the select-man's wife, or a tiny pair of kidskin boots for a pampered baby. Five pence half-penny was a fair price for a pair of "playne" shoes.

Although the farmers usually brought to the cobbler the hides which they had tanned, there was sometimes, at a distance from the town, a tannery where the disagreeable, tedious process was done for them. When the summer breeze was in the wrong direction, townsfolk were not sure that a tannery was an improvement.

There might also be a potter's shop, where housewives could purchase earthenware dishes of all sorts. The potter needed very little equipment to set up shop—only his wheel, operated by a foot treadle, and a supply of clay with which to make the serviceable dishes he sold—drinking mugs, jugs and bean pots. Near by there might be a joiner's shop where the local carpenter made and mended furniture, and there would surely

be a blacksmith's where farmers could have their horses and oxen shod.

Along the brook that meandered through the town, the miller set up his gristmill, damming the stream to make a waterfall to turn his great wooden wheel. Here the farmers brought their grain, rye or maize or wheat, to be ground into flour. Near by, using the same water power, there might be a sawmill to which the farmers would haul their logs and save themselves the heavy labor of sawing them into boards. Another mill which was set up early in almost every village was the fulling mill, which took over the final process of pounding and shrinking the woolen cloth which housewives had woven at home.

There was sure to be a tavern, which served not only as a place where a traveler could stop for a meal and a night's rest and where his horse could be "baited" or fed, but also as a warm and cheerful gathering place where the men of the village could meet for a glass of hot cider and an hour or two of good conversation. The tavern was the link that kept the village people in touch with the world outside. The latest letter, brought on horseback by the post, was read aloud; the week-old newspaper passed from hand to hand; and most important of all, the village men argued and debated. In this way the farmer in a remote village was aware of and came to be keenly interested in the changes taking place in the colonies.

City Life

A visitor from a small New England village must have found his head spinning when he visited the great town of Boston. In 1750, according to one visitor, Boston had three thousand houses, most of them wooden, two-story buildings, but some of brick, large and elegant. There were twelve meeting houses, and three churches, a fine two-story market, a handsome brick Town House, and shops of all kinds—tailors and milliners, jewelers and goldsmiths, cleaning and dyeing establishments, and barbers. The harbor, thronged with sailing ships from every port in the world, was guarded at its entrance by "a strong castle of a hundred guns built upon an island." Its busy wharves stretched in rows from the shore and were lined with warehouses and shops.

Visitors from other cities were less impressed by Boston. It was, in reality, an overgrown town. It had never been laid out according to plan, as had Philadelphia, but had grown from a small community clustered close, like any village, for safety and neighborliness. It had, and still has, one pride, its Common, fifty acres in the center of the town where the cows of all the citizens grazed freely as late as 1840.

Streets still followed the ancient cowpaths. John Drayton, a Southerner who visited Boston in 1793, left us an interesting description of them:

> *Few lamps assist the passenger through the streets by night, and if ever they were necessary in any place, they certainly are in this. For the streets are crooked, and narrow; paved from side to side with rough stones, extremely disagreeable, and inconvenient to those who walk them ... In many streets there are no railings or posts, to defend one from carriages, which are incessantly traveling them. Carts, wagons, drays, trucks, wheelbarrows, and porters are continually obstructing the passage in these streets ... I have seen a porter with a little hand cart pursuing his destination on the street, with the utmost unconcern, at the risk of being crippled, or having his cart crushed to pieces by a carriage which was thundering in his ears.*

Boston had been forced from its Puritan narrowness by the royal governors. There were now churches of many denominations, and another visitor, Brissot de Warville, was impressed by the fact that the ministers lived "in such harmony that they supply each other's places when any one is detained from his pulpit."

The vast wealth which flowed into Boston, and into other New England ports such as Salem, Massachusetts; Portsmouth, New Hampshire; Providence and Newport, Rhode Island, had been accumulated in shipbuilding and in rum and molasses trade, and often in African slaves. It made possible a very different life from any the early settlers could have dreamed. The royal governors who made their homes in Boston brought

Professionally a fine silversmith, Paul Revere is famous for having warned Lexington citizens of the coming of the British forces during the Revolution. (Museum of Fine Arts, Boston)

Both the silver cream pitcher (left) and the sugar bowl were his work. (Metropolitan Museum of Art)

A piece of embroidery, as detailed as a painting, of elegant parishioners arriving at Boston's Old South Church in 1756. (American Antiquarian Society)

with them from England their own wealth and pride, and set an example of a luxury that country villages could not even imagine. The governors built handsome mansions of brick, with as many as twenty-six rooms, and these were soon copied by wealthy Boston merchants who longed to see in Boston all the grandeur of Europe. In these mansions were elegant dining rooms and drawing rooms, where ladies and gentlemen in satin and laces and powdered wigs swayed through the minuet in the mirrored light of hundreds of candles. There were carved and paneled walls of mahogany and teakwood, marble mantels, and floors with mosaics of inlaid satinwood. There were elaborate hangings embroidered with peacocks and fruits and flowers.

The men and women who shared the privileged society which revolved around the royal governor adopted all the habits and styles of the English court, and they in turn set the styles for the lesser city folk, the tradesmen and their wives. Gone was the slightest trace of Puritan soberness. Boston rivaled the South in the luxury and lavishness of its dress. Every ship returning to England carried orders for the costliest of fabrics, for "a substantial silk, trimmed rich," "one fine cloth suit lined with scarlet," "pearl-colored silk hose," "flowered damask shoes," "colored kid gloves." Over and over again, orders specified that these things must be "fine ... of the best quality ... in the latest fashion." Nothing but the finest would do.

It must have been frustrating to Boston ladies who craved the latest fashions to wait weeks and months for letters and reports from London. But sometimes they could view, for a small fee, the latest "fashions baby" displayed by a modish dressmaker. These "babies," imported from London and dressed in the latest styles, were the first real dolls brought to American shores, and they were intended not as toys for little girls but as models for their mothers to admire and study.

Wigs made their appearance in Boston near the end of the seventeenth century and soon found their way to other New England towns. At first they were ridiculed and preached against, but before many years no gentleman dared to show himself in public without one. Even laborers who could not wear wigs at their daily work donned them on the Sabbath. They look so uncomfortable that we are glad to hear of one man who had reason to be grateful for his wig. An elderly Scotsman in Maine was caught in an Indian raid and pursued by a savage intent on his scalp. The Indian, overtaking his victim, reached gleefully for the man's hair and was terror-stricken when the scalp came off in his hand and the apparently scalped Scotsman bounded away to safety.

But Boston set the pace in more than its fashions. The brick mansions housed extensive and valuable libraries. Choral and instrumental music enriched the lives of the people. Boston schools set a high standard for the colonies. Bostonians were proud of their city.

A "fashions baby" of the 18th century. (Shelburne Museum)

North Haven Memorial Library
North Haven, Conn.

32887

The Dutch and the Quakers

3

"Thrice happy and ever to be envied little Burgh," wrote Washington Irving in his humorous history of New York. Certainly the Puritans on the rocky coast of New England must have envied the Dutch their cozy life on the fertile little island of Manhattan. To begin with, the Dutch were happy people, already blessed with peaceful, industrious and thrifty dispositions. And their settlement was carefully planned from the start to reduce to a minimum the hardships of the New World. They never faced starvation. They were able to bring with them from Holland plenty of food, tools, furniture, warm clothing, and many small comforts to keep them contented.

Unlike the New Englanders, the Dutch did not come to America to found a permanent home. The first settlers were attracted by the seemingly unlimited wealth of furs which Henry Hudson had reported, and they intended to make quick fortunes and return to Holland. Their settlement was a trading post. They found the Indians more than willing to exchange beaver skins for the trinkets they offered, and if the trinkets failed, unscrupulous traders did not hesitate to offer brandy and guns. Furs were collected at the trading post of Albany, 170 miles up the Hudson River, and shiploads of beaver skins and timber sailed regularly from the little port of New Amsterdam. The traders made their fortunes, but many of them fell in love with the pleasant new land and decided to stay.

To encourage permanent settlers, the West India Company in Holland gave huge tracts of lands to wealthy men known as patroons. These men in turn financed the voyage for small farmers and tradesmen who bound themselves to work for the patroons and to pay rent for the land they gave them. The relationship was very much like that of the old feudal barons and their serfs. Perhaps it was just as well that not many patroons actually settled in New Netherlands. The most famous of these was Kilaen Van Rensselaer, who built his manor far up the Hudson near Albany.

NIEUW AMSTERDAM

*A double-door kept the
Dutch housewife in touch
with her neighbors but
out of reach of rooting
pigs.*

*Left: Manhattan skyline
in the seventeenth
century. (Metropolitan
Museum of Art)*

Later the West India Company went still further and offered free passage
and free land to any settlers who would make their homes in the new
colony. Presently small *boweries,* or farms, spread across to Long Island
and along the opposite shore of the Hudson River in what is now New
Jersey.

A Dutch Bowery

The typical Dutch farmhouse on a bowery was long and low and widespread, built of wood or of fieldstone. The foundation of such a farmhouse
was carefully designed to make a cool dry cellar for storing the family
supply of food. There were kept the bins of vegetables, the great round
cheeses, the barrels of salt pork and pickled pigs' feet, and the vast quantities of pickles and preserves and jams put up by the housewife. On the
first floor was the spacious, comfortable kitchen or family room, and a
parlor or spare bedroom, and behind these there might be a small milk
room and a spinning room. The bedrooms were on the low second floor,
and above these, under the long sloping roof, was the garret, festooned
with dried vegetables. Often the garret contained a special small chimney
chamber where hams could be hung and cured by the smoke which rose
from the fireplace below.

The town houses in New Amsterdam were more often built of brick, with gables notched like steps and decorated with black brick or with iron work. English colonists were astonished to see the gable ends of Dutch houses facing the streets. Actually this was an example of Dutch thrift, for the water which dripped from the long roofs was collected in rain barrels in the yards. Chimneys were wide, with more steps built inside, so that a small boy could easily climb the gables, and scramble down the chimneys to clean them.

A special feature of Dutch houses in both town and country was the little *stoep* which became our stoop, a wide high doorstep with benches built on each side, on which the family spent the long evenings, the women knitting, the men smoking, ready for a pleasant chat with any passer-by. Another sociable feature was the double door, with upper and lower section separately hinged, so that the upper half could be left invitingly open while the lower section kept out unwanted callers such as stray dogs and swine. The upper half was sure to be decorated by a much-polished brass knocker.

The airy low-raftered family rooms of these houses were comfortably furnished with handsome heavy tables and ample-sized chairs well suited to the plump figures of the Dutch settlers. The most important item was a large cupboard known as a *kas* which a bride brought to her new home already filled with an abundant supply of snowy linen. Beds were likely to be invisible, built into alcoves or cupboards behind doors which were shut during the day, and sometimes even during the night. They were furnished with two deep feather beds, actually huge quilts, between which a person could sleep blissfully on the coldest night.

Dutch houses were far more colorful than New England homes. The great fireplace was often decorated with blue and white tiles with pictures of Bible scenes. Chairs were studded with brass nails, and cupboards and walls were enhanced with gaily-painted pictures. Windows sometimes contained one or two panes of bright-colored glass, and they were always hung with freshly laundered curtains. Shelves displayed the family pewter and the blue and white Delft china. Color also flaunted itself in the neat flower beds which the housewives planted outside their doors.

As in the old country, farmers soon had the long arms of windmills turning atop the hills of their new land.

The Little Dutch Burgh Becomes New York

When the famous Peter Stuyvesant sailed into the harbor of New Amsterdam in 1647 to be the new governor, he found a thriving little town, copied as much as possible after the city in Holland. There was a counting house built of stone, where business was conducted, and a stout little fort. There were rows of neat, gabled brick houses, and a number of these had shops in their front rooms. There were common pastures for the sheep and cattle. There was even a small canal flowing down Broad Street, built by erecting dykes along the sides of a ditch. Several small bridges spanned this canal, and one of these was the favorite meeting place at which the burghers leaned on the wooden rails and conducted their business. Another favorite gathering place was under a great elm tree before the

11.

tavern named "der Halle," where the older Dutchmen could sit on summer afternoons, puffing on their long-stemmed pipes.

Windmills topped the highest hills, and the huge revolving arms that terrified the *wilden*, as the Indians were called, were useful not only to turn the grindstones in the mill below, but, when not in use, as signals. By certain positions of the arms, much like the semaphore code today, the people could be warned of an attack. To guard the inhabitants there was also a "rattle watch" of eight men, who patrolled the streets all night, sounding their wooden rattles and rapping on every door as they passed to reassure the sleepers that all was well.

During the time that New Amsterdam was merely a trading post, no one bothered to establish a church or a school. Sabbath services were held in the loft of a windmill. But some time before Stuyvesant, a "Dominie," or pastor, had arrived from Holland, and the people had built him a small church. Although the Dutch church did not impose on its people the rigid Sabbath of the Puritans, the townsfolk were expected to attend services, and men were not allowed to work or children to play on the streets during the time of worship. Education, however, was much neglected. The town had still not provided a schoolhouse for the schoolmaster who had come on the same boat with the Dominie.

Under Peter Stuyvesant the town flourished. With very little trouble he added to New Netherlands the Swedish settlement along the Delaware River. He established a fire department and a hospital and granted more privileges to his council of burghers. He made an uneasy peace with the Indians who were raging to revenge the injustices they had suffered. He tried to reach an agreement with the English who were coming nearer and nearer in Connecticut and on Long Island.

But the English had never recognized any Dutch claims to the territory they still considered part of Virginia. In 1668 four English warships sailed into the harbor of New Amsterdam. Peter Stuyvesant tried gallantly to rouse his burghers to defend their city. But the placid burghers were

Each man carrying a rattle as well as a lantern, the "rattle watch" sets out to patrol the streets of New Amsterdam.

not soldiers by nature. They knew that the little fort on the Battery had only a few guns. Rather than see their pleasant homes destroyed, they forced their governor to surrender without a struggle. Most of them felt that their lives would be changed very little under English rule, and they were right. New Amsterdam was renamed New York, and the neighboring territory across the river was christened New Jersey. An English governor came to live in the city's White Hall. But Dutchmen continued to speak their native tongue for almost a hundred years, and only very gradually did their own customs merge with those of the English.

Left: To bed in a cupboard! Dutch settlers slept warmly between feather mattresses in alcoves.

Burgher and Goede Vrouw

Washington Irving commented that the burgomasters were chosen by weight. Certainly the Dutch loved to eat, and their good wives were noted as excellent cooks. The settlers soon developed a fondness for the corn puddings and suppawn which the Indians taught them to make, and in

57

A 17th-century view of the canal which later became Canal Street.
(New-York Historical Society)

addition their tables were loaded with game, with fruits and vegetables of their own raising, and with the most delicious pies and pastries. Guests were always welcome, and many houses kept, in addition to the bed in the company room, piles of furs or mattresses always ready for an unexpected crowd. Holidays were many and filled with gaiety. Country people especially delighted in the annual country fair, the Kermiss, at which farmers exhibited their cattle, exchanged their produce, and engaged in sports and merrymaking for days at a stretch. Town people had their sleighing parties and their dances and theaters and balls.

The Dutch burgher presented a colorful figure as he walked slowly from his shop or his office to his favorite coffeehouse. His velvet coat was cut in the latest style. His knickerbockers were baggier than those of the English, and his hat was wider, with curling plumes and feathers. He fancied the starched and elaborately pleated collar known as a ruff. His *goede Vrouw* was also dressed in the height of fashion, in satin or velvet gown, tight bodice with loose, short-sleeved jacket and dainty white undersleeves, and she wore a ruff even stiffer and wider than her husband's. Madam Knight, a visitor from Boston, wrote an interesting description of the women in New York:

> They wear French mouches which are like a cap and a head band in one, leaving their ears bare, which are set out with jewels of a large size and many in number. And their fingers hoop't with rings, some with large stones in them of many colors as were their pendants in their ears, which you should see very old women wear as well as young.

Farmers and lesser folk wore work clothes of linsey-woolsey or leather during the week, but on Sundays and holidays they imitated the well-to-do. Every Dutch wife donned as many petticoats as she could—a bride wore all the petticoats she owned at her wedding. Every woman wore apron and cap; a married woman was distinguished by a special "coif." Around her waist she wore a chatelaine, or clasp, of gold or silver or brass, hung with keys, pincushions, scissors and any other notion she might fancy, and on Sunday she added a fine prayer book.

The linens on sleeves and ruffs and collars and caps were kept immaculately white and crisply ironed, as were the curtains and napkins and all the household linen. On Sundays even the fireplace wore a trim little petticoat of starched linen. Dutch housewives have always been

Tin-covered wooden weather vane, taken from the first New Amsterdam Stadthuys (Town Hall) erected in 1642. (New-York Historical Society)

An old print showing the New Amsterdam Stadthuys, at the corner of Pearl Street and Coenties Slip, in 1679. (Museum of the City of New York)

famous for their spotless cleanliness, and this virtue was quite remarkable in colonial America. Peter Kalm, a visitor from Sweden, felt that they were "almost over-nice." He also commented that every woman over forty smoked a pipe, and he was especially amused at the way, in cold weather, they concealed warming pans beneath their voluminous petticoats and went to all sorts of trouble to refill them without anyone noticing. Dutch housewives, though they wanted to be kind to the *wilden,* shrank from inviting them into their houses, since the savages rubbed fish oil and grease on their bodies and seldom washed.

Dutch women were also surprisingly capable businesswomen, no doubt because Holland was far in advance of other countries in its belief in education for girls. Many housewives in New Amsterdam ran shops, and a few were successful traders in their own right.

The Dutch village of Albany must have been an especially happy place for boys and girls, who had a freedom that no other colony allowed. An English woman who wrote under the name Mrs. Grant, spent her childhood in the town and later wrote of the picnics, where the boys fished while the girls gathered wild strawberries or opened their little work baskets and busied themselves with embroidery or knitting, and where they all enjoyed a feast and went home singing through the twilight. In the winter there were sleighing parties on the frozen river, followed by gay little suppers. All boys from eight to eighteen enjoyed coasting down the long hills, and young men had a special sport of stealing turkeys for their bachelor parties at the tavern. But when a man married he had to give up coasting, and had to resign himself to watching his old friends sneak into his backyard to steal his turkeys.

When a boy fell in love, according to Mrs. Grant, he followed a certain pattern. Though he might have known his bride-to-be all his life, he still had to prove himself. He laid aside his gun and his fishing rod, asked his father for a canoe and a Negro servant, and set out as an independent trader into the wilderness. After a year of living with the savages, matching his wits with theirs, and enduring danger and bitter weather, a boy returned quite changed. He was now "master of himself." But there was more to be done. He went down to New York, sold his furs, bought a ship which he filled with flour and provisions, and sailed for the Bermudas, where he took on a cargo of rum, and sugar and molasses. After all this he was a man, usually about twenty-two years old, ready to claim his bride, to settle down and turn farmer—unless he had caught the fever of trading and decided to remain a trader for life.

Mrs. Grant also remembered that just before the Revolution the simple people of Albany were startled at seeing their first play, produced in a barn by a group of British officers. The townsfolk did not understand all the witty dialogue, but they were entranced at seeing the officers taking the parts of women, with hoop skirts and fans and painted faces. The old folks who objected that it was all a falsehood were scoffed at by the young. The beloved old Dominie, who objected most loudly, found on his doorstep a well-known hint—an old stick to push him away, a pair of old shoes and a dollar for a journey. Heartbroken at this joke of some

A Maypole was the center of gaiety on May Day.

thoughtless young people, he actually did leave his church, took ship for Holland, and vanished en route.

On the whole, however, the people of New Netherlands seem to have been unusually well-mannered and kindly. Their town records contain very few serious crimes, and their punishments were not so harsh nor so frequent as those of New England. They cared for the few poor in their midst by regular contributions in the church poor box. Though many of the wealthy families owned Negro slaves, they treated them indulgently and never sold them to other masters. When a child was born to a slave he was presented as a gift to a child in the family and the two grew up together in close friendship. A slave boy or girl understood perfectly that presently the white playmate would become master or mistress, but the affection and loyalty between the two sometimes lasted a lifetime.

George Washington's New York

In 1789 New York was chosen as the nation's first capital, and four years later the first Congress of the United States met in the city hall. The city that greeted President Washington had changed greatly from the little town governed by Peter Stuyvesant. The inauguration parade rode between cheering crowds along cobbled streets. The old lanterns which had once swung from every seventh house had been replaced with oil lamps on poles. There were splendid houses and fashionable shops which displayed the latest styles at high prices. There were fine public buildings, a hospital, a library, a poorhouse, a jail, and Columbia College, which boasted eighty students (the name had been quickly changed from King's College when the colonies revolted). There were factories and warehouses, and the harbor was thronged with ships from every country in the world.

Many of the streets still kept the names given them by the Dutch people in the early days. Maiden Lane was the path worn by the young girls on their way to wash clothes in the brook. Whitehall Street led to the White Hall, the mansion built by Governor Stuyvesant. Stone Street had been the first street to be paved with cobblestones. The Battery was still the site of the fort, and the most important street, the Breede Weg, had become Broadway. The Bowery was a part of Peter Stuyvesant's

In old New York, peddlers cried their wares, hawking everything from cattails to tea rusks. These vignettes of "Cries of New York" are taken from a silk scarf of the early 1800's. (Museum of the City of New York)

bouwerie, and no one needs to be told where Conyn's Island and Breuchelen once were.

Many things in the new capital would seem shocking to us today. There was no running water anywhere in the city. Not a single one of the imposing mansions had a bathtub. The city sewage disposal operated on a very elementary plan—every household dumped its garbage and slops into the gutter, and the city sanitation department was composed of hogs who rooted everywhere underfoot. And there must have been noise, for every visitor complained of it, and some called it deafening. Chimney sweeps, knife grinders, tinkers, ragmen, wood and water sellers, peddlers of all sorts kept up a constant racket, shouting their wares. Reckless horsemen paid no heed to pedestrians. Children ran shrieking in and out, almost under the wheels of coaches. And at any moment there was likely to be a street brawl, for the great harbor attracted a lawless crowd.

Yet there were also theaters and music halls where one could hear the finest music in the world. In 1789 New York already had about it the special excitement which visitors find there today. Because so many nationalities entered the harbor, New York had a cosmopolitan atmosphere quite different from Boston or Philadelphia. Along the busy waterfront, sailors jabbered in every language under the sun. In the fine mansions society was flavored with the elegant manners of European capitals. New York was truly the meeting place of many nations.

The Quakers Find a Home

The Quakers, like the Puritans, had broken away from the Church of England, but they went far beyond the Puritans in their beliefs. Their ideas were very startling to the people of that time. They held that since all men were equal before God, no man could set himself above his fellow men. Quakers refused to take off their hats even to the king, and they addressed everyone by the simple "thee" and "thou" generally used only for servants and children. Each man was free to understand the truth in his own way. There were no ministers in Quaker churches, and no sermons. There was not even a church service that Puritans could understand. The Friends, as they called themselves, merely met and sat together in silence, each worshiping in his own heart. From time to time one of them would be specially moved to break the silence to share some inspiration with the others. They felt no need for the sacraments of communion and baptism. They turned to the Bible as their only guide, and waited quietly for the "light within" to tell them what to do.

Such beliefs outraged almost everyone—Anglicans, Catholics and Puritans alike. Quakers were harshly persecuted in England and not welcomed anywhere in the colonies. Those who were rash enough to land in Boston suffered fines and imprisonment, whipping, and even death. It must be admitted that they did not suffer all this with meekness. They

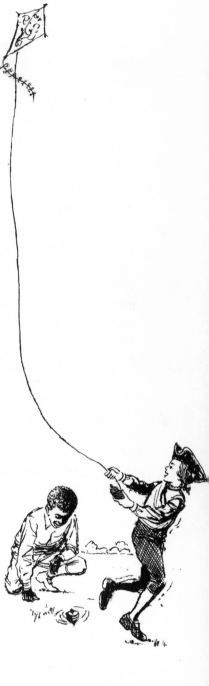

A white child plays with his slave companion.

63

Quakers riding to meeting in summer, from a contemporary travel book.
(New-York Historical Society)

loudly denounced Puritan beliefs, and some of them made spectacles of themselves and interrupted Puritan meetings. One Quaker and his wife were tied to a cart and whipped over the Massachusetts border five different times, and each time returned. Their consciences had convinced them that they must suffer this persecution till public opinion was aroused and their people were allowed to worship in peace. Mary Dyer, one of their number, was condemned to be hanged with two fellow Quakers, but was pardoned at the last moment and banished from Massachusetts instead. She deliberately came back again to certain death.

In England the Friends were fortunate to have as one of their leaders a man who was not only a devout Quaker but a businessman and a diplomat of remarkable talent. As the young son of an aristocrat, William Penn sacrificed a chance for a brilliant career to work for the Quaker cause. He failed to win a place for the Friends in England, so he used his influence at court to obtain a grant of land in the New World.

Penn set about the organization of his new settlement with care and skill. Every detail was planned in advance. Though the king's grant was vague, Penn did not try to claim a vast territory he could not use. He made an agreement with the Indians that he would purchase the amount of land he could cover in three days' walking. The Indians understood such an arrangement and respected the man who made it, and by this purchase Penn won many years of peace. The beautiful land he had obtained, the sober and industrious people he brought with him, and his own masterly planning guaranteed success from the very start.

City of Brotherly Love

Philadelphia was planned according to Quaker principles. Each man was to have space and freedom, and no man's house should be bigger than his neighbor's. The streets were laid out in rectangular order, crossing each other at right angles, with here and there space left for public parks. In William Penn's plan the government, too, was based on the Quaker faith. Every man could vote, every religion was welcome, and capital punishment was limited to just two crimes, treason and murder.

In their new city the Quakers tried to live quietly, peaceably, and moderately. They did not condemn worldly goods as did the Puritans, but they did not set themselves above each other by any special display. When they prospered, as they very shortly did, they did not flaunt their wealth. Their clothes, their houses, and their furniture were all of good quality, but they preferred simple lines and sober colors.

It is not surprising that the Quakers very soon began to speak out against the system of slavery at a time when Christians in other colonies could see nothing wrong in it. The Pennsylvania Assembly prohibited new slaves from coming into the colony, and Quakers who owned slaves were urged to grant them freedom. Quakers also were among the first colonists to be concerned with the education of both Negro and Indian children, and many devout Friends dedicated their lives to preaching and teaching among their dark-skinned brothers.

William Penn's town grew rapidly. Shipbuilding and trade brought great wealth to the merchants, and an ever-increasing population brought shops and industries, taverns and public buildings. By the middle of the eighteenth century, fifty years after William Penn's death, Philadelphia was the largest city in the English colonies. Much of the simplicity and soberness of the Quaker town had been forgotten in these busy years, but the Quaker influence still remained strong.

In the eighteenth century Philadelphia found another outstanding leader, Benjamin Franklin, who was not a Quaker but a Bostonian who chose Philadelphia for his home. Besides his amazing ability as an inventor, publisher and businessman, Franklin had a deep concern for the welfare of all men. Under his inspiration Philadelphia led the colonies in the establishment of many civic organizations—a fire department, a humane prison far in advance of any the world had ever known, a

A hand-painted box, a common wedding gift to Pennsylvania German couples. The inscription reads: "Oh, how happy my love will be when we marry." (Cooper Union)

remarkable hospital which cared for the insane as well as the sick, a plan
for medical care for the poor, a library, and a philosophical society that
promoted scientific research and study throughout the colonies.

Benjamin Franklin's Philadelphia must have been a happy place to
live in, though the Quaker founders would not have approved of the
elegant social life or the beautiful mansions. Formal banquets, beginning
at four in the afternoon, included far too many courses. There were
sumptuous balls and parties, and masquerades with the most elaborate
costumes.

Not all the fun was confined to the mansions. Taverns such as the
Coach and Horses and the Penny Pot Inn catered to gourmets of all
classes. And Philadelphians had a passion for joining. There were clubs
of every imaginable kind—social clubs, "glutton" clubs, fire companies,
library clubs, musical and debating societies. Besides meeting together to
share the same interests, members worked together to improve their city.
Moreover, people were suddenly waking up to the wonderful scientific
discoveries taking place in the world. They flocked to lectures on chemis-

try, electricity, anatomy and astronomy. Though many of Penn's ideals had been forgotten, he would have seen much to please him in the city he had founded.

Melting Pot

Many other groups of colonists followed the Dutch and Quakers into the Middle Colonies, and each made its own contribution to American life. The Swedish settlers on the Delaware River introduced the log cabin, which was used everywhere on the Western frontier and which became the symbol of the American pioneer. The Catholic colonists in Maryland were the first to pass a definite law guaranteeing religious freedom in their colony. The French Huguenots brought to America a love of beauty which showed itself in the flower gardens which sprang up wherever they settled, and in the beautiful handicrafts, embroidery and silver which they created. The Jews who came to New York and to Georgia and South Carolina brought an age-old culture and love of learning.

Colonists also came by the thousands from Germany, many of them indentured servants. They moved beyond Philadelphia into the rich farming country where their neatly kept farms and large red barns are still part of the landscape. They clung to their own ways and to the language mistakenly called Pennsylvania Dutch. Among them were scholars and musicians who brought to America the finest of Old World music.

Pushing far beyond the settled farms into the Indian territory to the west came the Scotch-Irish, hardy, restless Scots who had lived for scarcely a generation in Ireland. They established a new frontier toward the Allegheny Mountains and Kentucky. There they became true backwoodsmen—fiercely independent, building their log cabins with their own hands, adopting the fringed hunting shirts and deerhide moccasins of the Indians—expert riflemen, and, as they proved in the War for Independence, staunch American patriots.

Women of all classes shopped in the street markets of the 1790's.

A microscope of the early 1800's. (Colonial Williamsburg)

The Goodwife at Home

4

In the autumn of 1802 a young man and his wife and year-old child sailed from Portsmouth, New Hampshire, along the coast of Maine, and up the Penobscot River to Bangor. Leaving the boat, they set out on foot along a blazed trail in the forest, carrying the baby in their arms by turns. After thirteen miles they came to a small settlement with a gristmill, and there met a boy who had brought grain to the mill on horseback and who was willing to lend his horse to the exhausted wife. They went on into the wilderness, through a damp chilling snowfall, with no road of any kind, over ground treacherous with streams and swamps. For the last eight miles the young wife, drenched, shivering, utterly weary, was "as willing to die as to live." At the end of the day she saw for the first time the home her husband had prepared for her—the clearing of raw tree stumps, the solitary log cabin, the garden with the first ripened ears of the corn he had planted in the spring. There were no neighbors. Alone in this tiny cabin the little family was to spend all winter. In the spring they might hope for other homesteads and new faces.

There is nothing remarkable about this story. It was a commonplace journey, duplicated times without number in settlements from Maine to Georgia and westward to Ohio and Kentucky and beyond, wherever women followed their husbands into the wilderness and shared cold and danger and loneliness and hard labor to make a home for their children. But there are tales of real heroism as well—stories of women who loaded a musket while their husbands fired from a slit in the long wall into a howling mob of Indians, or of women who could aim the musket themselves if need be, or of women who gave birth to children on the trail, miles from the nearest settlement. These women would never in their lives know the feel of a high-heeled slipper or a powdered wig. They were the pioneers in homespun petticoats who helped to make American history.

Diaries kept in 1775 by two young sisters, Abigail and Elizabeth Foote, give us a vivid picture of daily life in a colonial home. Almost every day each girl spun two pounds of flax. They spun, they "spooled a piece," they washed, scoured, made cheese, sanded the parlor, knit worsted stockings, hatcheled and carded wool and flax. For recreation they went cherrying or to a quilting, keeping their fingers busy while their tongues wagged. Reading the diaries, one wonders where they found hours enough in the day, and also whether they ever rebelled at the never-ending round of chores. Perhaps not, for they had never seen their mother or any of their young friends with idle hands.

A kettle with legs, a skillet, a gridiron, and a toaster are a few of the household utensils the little girl must learn to use.

Like Abigail and Elizabeth, every colonial girl, from the time she could walk, was trained in the skills of housekeeping. She might not be troubled with much book learning. But when a young bride crossed the threshold of her own home, she did so with confidence, taking with her a dowry of linens spun and woven by her own hand, and a sure knowledge of how to use every new pot and kettle that hung by her hearth.

She needed to bring to her new home, as well, patience and strong muscles. The labor of the colonial housewife was backbreaking drudgery. In a frontier settlement, housekeeping was only part of her duties; she helped to clear the land and build the house and plant the crops as well. Even when she lived in a village of snug, comfortable houses, her daily tasks filled every hour from sunrise to long after sunset.

Hasty Pudding and Pumpkin Pie

Most of the housewife's day was consumed in preparing meals. Every step of the preparation had to be done the hard way, with heavy, awkward equipment. Someone has written that the great kettles seem more

A long day's work by this crude method could yield the housewife as many as 200 candles.

suitable for giants to handle than for women. Yet in the course of her day every woman filled and lifted and toted and scoured them in her struggle to provide food for her family. And when her goodman came in from a morning of chopping and hoeing, sniffed at the fragrance that filled the kitchen, and stole a peek into the bubbling pot, what was he likely to find?

Chiefly hasty pudding. For the first hundred years and more, the mainstay of the colonists' diet was the Indian corn which Governor Bradford of Plymouth colony called "more precious than silver." It grew abundantly and it was very nourishing. Indians on the warpath had been known to travel great distances on a daily ration of just three spoonfuls of powdered cornmeal, which they called "nocake," mixed with a little water. Roger Williams, when he was an outcast in the wilderness, often made "a good meal" of a single spoonful. Certainly whole families thrived on a diet of corn and little else, day after day, year after year, for all of their lives. Joel Barlow, who wrote a poem in praise of hasty pudding, spoke for all New Englanders when he said, "All my bones are made of Indian corn."

Just as we do today, the settlers relished most the fresh corn, wrapped in its own husks and roasted in the coals. But this was a luxury. The main part of the crop had to be saved for winter, the kernels dried and ground into meal to make the daily bread. In the days before gristmills, colonists adopted the Indian method of pounding the parboiled kernels in a hollow stone. Then they learned to construct Indian mortars by hollowing out stumps of trees. Above the stump they would swing a heavy block of wood from the top of a pliant young tree. After the housewife pounded the pestle block down into the mortar, the tree sprang up again, saving her the labor of lifting the pestle. This invention was called a "sweep and mortar mill," and it could be heard for some distance, so that a woman would feel less lonely as she heard the thump of her neighbor's mill echoing her own. Later families did not need to grind their own corn, but carried it to a miller who had set up a water mill or a windmill. But as late as 1800, settlers in remote villages in Maine and other frontier colonies were still using the old Indian mortars.

The usual way of cooking the corn meal was to mix it with water or milk and boil it for hours, with much stirring, till it formed a rather solid pudding. This was Joel Barlow's hasty pudding, but for the cook there was nothing hasty about it. Most colonial families ate such a pudding twice every day of the year. For the main course it was served with milk or gravy, and for dessert it was sweetened with maple syrup. If there was more than one course, the pudding was served first. Corn flour also made a crusty bread, sometimes studded with wild huckleberries or apple slices, and the famous "johnny cake" baked in the chimney oven. And Indian corn had a special surprise in store for boys and girls. In 1639 Governor Winthrop wrote that when corn was parched it turned inside out and was "white and floury within." One of the earliest gadgets was a long-handled corn popper not unlike ours today.

To vary the everlasting corn diet there were beans and pumpkins, two other plants the colonists adopted from the Indians. Think of the debt we owe the first housewife who delighted her family with a pumpkin pie! All through the winter, festoons of dried pumpkin chunks hung from the rafters on long strings, and added a cheery note of color to the family kitchen. When a housewife wanted to make a pie, she had only to reach up and break off what she needed.

Although there was plenty of game in the forests, the guns of the early hunters were so clumsy that it was a lucky shot that actually brought down a deer or a rabbit. When a fortunate hunter brought in a large roast, there was no way to preserve the meat, so he shared it in a neighborhood feast. Fish was easier to catch, and the ocean was teeming with cod, mackerel and bass, lobsters of enormous size, and oysters and

Above: A hanging candlestick. It was adjustable for reading.
Right: An iron betty lamp that gave a smoky light from the wick
at its lip.
(Metropolitan Museum of Art)

clams. In inland brooks a man could catch a barrel of eels in one night; boiled in wine and spices they were a favorite dish.

After a few years in a settlement a housewife had more variety for her table. Fruit trees sprang up quickly on American soil, and the familiar carrots and turnips and onions appeared in every garden patch. There were also good things just for the picking—wild strawberries and raspberries and other berries, walnuts and chestnuts.

In England and in Europe people were accustomed to wine and beer with their meals. The colonists took to water in a gingerly way as a last resort. As soon as the first apple crops were harvested they began to press the cider that would be the chief beverage on their tables at every meal. Popular at house-raisings, funerals, and other sociable gatherings, was a mixture of rum and cider known as flip. For a cheering hot drink a special toddy iron, like a long poker, was heated red-hot in the fireplace coals and thrust into a noggin of cider or flip. Tea and coffee were unknown in America until after 1700.

Lug-Pole and Brick Oven

For two hundred years housewives everywhere in every colony cooked their meals exactly as the first settlers in Plymouth had done. All the cooking and baking was done at the huge fireplace. The array of iron gadgets which stood about the hearth changed very little through the years. There were the huge kettles, some of them holding fifteen gallons, and it does seem an undertaking for a giant to hoist one of these onto the

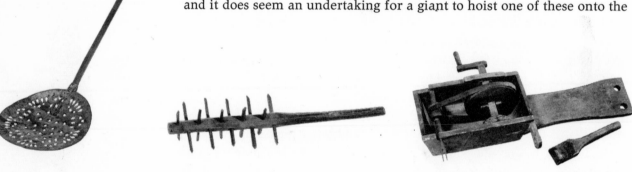

Copper cream skimmer (left), wooden egg-beater (center), and an apple-parer (right) which the housewife worked by turning the apple on a prong while paring it with the scraper. (New-York Historical Society)

lug-pole in the back of a vast fireplace. Often it took two people and a crowbar to lift a full kettle to the pole or to remove it, and the first poles of green wood were constantly burning through and spilling the precious contents into the ashes. A woman must have felt that she had a wonderfully modern kitchen when she acquired a strong iron crane that would swing the kettle out from the fire and allow her to manage it by herself. A meat stew could be preserved for several days by keeping it slowly simmering at the back of the hearth, from time to time throwing in more vegetables and handfuls of spices and herbs. Many housewives kept a small betty lamp which could be lowered on a chain into the depths of a bubbling kettle so that they could see how a stew was progressing.

Turkeys and geese were hung by strings over the fire, and the string kept constantly twirling for even browning. Roasts of meat were cooked on a large spit, something like our barbecue. The twirling of the string or the turning of the spit was a proper chore for a child, but in the inns of a later period dogs were trained to work a small treadmill which kept the spit turning. There were also iron toasters and broilers and grates which could be set close to the blazing coals, and a "bake oven," which was a kettle on legs.

Surprisingly, colonial dames learned how to turn out all sorts of delicious pies and cakes and cookies from the small brick ovens built into the side of the chimney. On baking day a hot fire was built inside the deep oven. When it was reduced to ashes, the ashes were swept out and the pies and cakes set deftly in by means of a long-handled shovel. Baking was a laborious process, and a large supply was made at a time. An old-timer in Peacham, Vermont, recalled that as many as sixty mince pies would be baked in a day and frozen till needed. Recipes of those days were complicated and dealt with large quantities; a single cake might call for a dozen eggs and two pounds of flour.

Autumn was the busiest time of all for the housewife, and for the children as well, for every pair of hands was needed to make ready for the winter. Quinces, pears, plums, peaches and berries of all sorts were preserved in huge crocks or boiled into rich spicy jams and marmalades. Apples were peeled and sliced and strung up to dry for winter pies, or boiled in the kettles to make vast barrels of applesauce or apple butter. Meat and fish were salted down or smoked and packed into barrels. Cheese was pressed into flat wheels. In addition, a housewife prided

Above: A waffle iron with a hearts-and-diamonds pattern. (New-York Historical Society)

Right: A lemon squeezer made of wood, and an iron that was heated by means of a piece of hot metal placed inside it. (Colonial Williamsburg)

Below: Working like a tiny guillotine, this instrument cored and split apples. (New-York Historical Society)

herself on a store of fancy pickles and relishes, made from such unlikely plants as nasturtium buds, green walnuts, barberries, marigolds, roses, violets and peonies.

The Board is Spread

Like the Pilgrims at Plymouth, pioneer families for two hundred years ate their simple meals at long boards or trestles set up before the fireplace and spread with a clean linen cloth. The head of the family sat at the table, perhaps in the only chair in the house. His wife sat beside him on a stool or bench. There were no highchairs, and young children simply stood at the end of the board, or even respectfully behind their parents, and ate, quietly and without speaking, whatever was passed to them. Since the meal usually consisted of but one dish, this was not really an ordeal, except for the long Puritan prayer. The meal vanished quickly. In the first years, with so much to be done, eating was a solemn business and no occasion for merriment.

There were no dishes in the first log houses. A frontier woman might carry with her a cherished cup, perhaps, or a pair of spoons. Early settlers in every colony made their dishes out of the only material at hand. Wooden tableware of all kinds was known as "treen," doubtless because it was made from a tree. A wooden trencher, which was merely a flat board with a hollow carved in it, usually served two people. Everyone ate with fingers. Forks were unheard of in Puritan colonies; even a wealthy family would boast only one for the master of the house. Knives were unnecessary, since every man carried a hunting knife in his pocket. As soon as there was a supply of pewter in the colonies a family made its own spoon mold, since the metal was easily cracked and bent, and spoons could be melted down and molded over again.

An interesting Puritan institution was the large saltcellar which was the most valuable possession on the family table. It was made of pewter, or sometimes of silver, and it stood prominently near the head of the table. By old English custom, it was a mark of distinction for the master and important guests, such as the minister, to sit "above the salt." Children and unimportant folk took their places below.

As towns became settled and more prosperous, the dining tables of the colonists took on a very different appearance. Meals became more leisurely, with several courses and varied kinds of food. Everyday tables were still set with treen or with a reddish-brown pottery and pewter. For company the silver spoons were brought out, and the silver candlesticks. Displayed in the cupboard were china plates and dishes imported from England, mainly white stoneware and blue and white delft. Occasionally there was a cherished piece of Canton porcelain from China. Glassware of all kinds was plentiful after the Revolution, though little of it was made in the colonies. Forks replaced fingers now, though it was still customary to do most of one's eating with a knife. There was a new interest in table manners. A popular little book for young people, entitled *The School of Good Manners,* reminded children to "Bite not thy bread, but break it," to "Take not salt with a greasy knife," and "When helping your superior to an article he shall ask for, throw it not at him." Children sat at the table now with their elders, but they were still expected to eat respectfully and to speak only when spoken to. Trading ships brought delicacies from distant lands, though at first these appeared only on the tables of city folk. Besides the fragrant spices, there were oranges and raisins and figs, almonds, and delicious chocolate. City shops carried a variety of "sweetmeats" and "comfits"—candied lemon peel, angelica, sugared corrinder seeds, and glazed almonds.

About 1714 the first tea came to Boston, and the ladies took it to their hearts. It was expensive and housewives tried all sorts of substitutes. An old cookbook advises, "The first leaves of the common currant bush, gathered at once and dried on tin, can hardly be distinguished from green tea." But colonial ladies could distinguish; only Chinese tea would do for

Right: The children will remain standing "below the salt" (the bowl in the center of the table), but the pilgrim goodwife will sit beside her husband and share his wooden trencher.

Below: A well sweep.

fashionable tea tables. With the tea came the first china cups, delicate and without handles, imported from France. Few hostesses could boast a set of them. When a lady went to a tea party she carried her own tiny cup, saucer and spoon. She poured the hot tea from the cup and sipped daintily from the saucer. Every housewife longed for white sugar to serve, and she ordered one "cone" of it a year to reserve for festive occasions. It came in clear, rocklike chunks weighing nine or ten pounds, and had to be painstakingly cut into dainty pieces with a special sugar cutter.

While the old hasty pudding still appeared daily on country boards, in the cities the candle-lit tables were laden with rich and varied dishes, following each other in course after course. Famous inns served banquets of staggering abundance. The founders of our republic were hearty eaters. Benjamin Franklin, Thomas Jefferson, and other prominent men of their time sat down to magnificent dinners which included soup and oysters, several varieties of fish, roasted turkey, chicken, duck and goose, beef and mutton, beautiful molded jellies, plum puddings, pies and cakes and tarts—all this in one meal! Accompanying the courses were great bowls of hot flip or fragrant spiced punch.

Flax spinning.

An explanation in a child's reader tells how hemp is made into cloth. (New York Public Library)

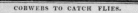

COBWEBS TO CATCH FLIES.   33

THE WALK.

(In Words of Five and Six Letters.)

BOY.

There is a field full of nettles.

PAPA.

No, not so, it is hemp.

BOY.

What is that for, papa?

PAPA.

To make cloth of; the stalk has a tough peel on it, and that peel is what they make thread of. The thread they weave, and make strong cloth.

Candle Dipping

The soft and lovely light of candles was earned only by long, tiresome and unpleasant labor. Collecting the tallow was a year-round care, since every precious drop of fat or suet from beef or deer, even bear's grease, was carefully hoarded. In the fall this unsavory mass was added to boiling water in huge kettles, and boiled and skimmed, boiled and skimmed, for several days till a clear tallow was obtained.

On candle-dipping day a hot fire had to be kept burning all day long under the kettle of melted tallow. Two long poles were laid across chair backs, and across these poles rested the candle rods, sticks about eighteen inches long. From each rod were looped several wicks of twisted hemp. The housewife dipped a rod of wicks at a time into the hot kettle, hung it back to harden and cool, then dipped it and hung it again, over and over, till the candles slowly fattened. It is said that a good worker could make two hundred candles in a day. Since the racks had to be hung well away from the fire, sometimes even in a lean-to, imagine the number of trips from rack to kettle these two hundred candles required!

A happy discovery of the colonists was that the little grayish berries which grew in abundance along the coast could be boiled down into a pure clear tallow. Bayberry candles kept hard and straight through the summer heat, and in the winter the clean spicy fragrance they gave off when extinguished brought a hint of summer into the room. A pleasant custom was to light bayberry candles when callers were expected and snuff them out, so that their fragrance lingered in the room as a welcome.

In time the colonists devised candle molds which saved the housewife much labor, since she had only to pour the melted tallow into the long tin cylinders. Sometimes this task was taken over by candlemakers who traveled from house to house carrying their own molds. But hand-dipped bayberry candles were cherished by housewives, and are still much loved in New England today.

Scrubbing and Scouring

Another tedious and disagreeable use for collected grease was the making of soap. Housewives kept ashes from the hearth in a "leach barrel." From time to time they poured water through the ashes and allowed it to trickle out the bottom into a small tub, making homemade lye. Lye from about six bushels of ashes, added to twenty pounds of grease, boiled together and constantly stirred over an outdoor fire, made one small barrel of soft, jellylike soap.

Washday was a burdensome affair of hauling and heating water. The snowy white napkins and tablecloths which were a housewife's pride were earned only by painful scrubbing, especially in the days before forks. In addition, there was the daily cleaning of the kettles, the scouring away of grease and black soot with sand or rushes. The hearth had to be kept immaculate, and the floor swept and covered with a fine layer of clean sand which served in place of a rug.

In cool weather all water for family bathing also had to be hauled and heated. A hot bath in a tub before the roaring fire must have been

This painting of a flax scutching bee was made about 1860, but the procedure had not changed much from colonial days. (National Gallery of Art) Below: A comb for straightening out tangled flax fibers. (Old Sturbridge Village)

a real luxury, and we can scarcely blame our ancestors if perhaps this was not a very frequent affair.

Snails, Superstition and Common Sense

It was the responsibility of the housewife to keep the medicine chest well stocked with remedies, for the colonial home was self-sufficient even to providing its own drug store. Most of the ingredients she found in her own garden. She knew how to make palsy drops, snail water, pokeberry plasters, and how to brew teas from sage, tansy, wormwood, catnip and other herbs. Violets were soothing for fevers and sore throats. Dill cured hiccups or "yexing." And pinks "do wonderfully cheer and comfort the heart."

Not all the ancient benefits sound so appealing. Some of the recipes brought from England and Europe called for horrifying and disgusting ingredients such as ground snails, worms and toads. The more unpleasant the cure, the more faith people seemed to have in it. For deafness, roasted hedgehog fat was dropped into the ear and covered with black wool. The blood from a male cat's ear mixed with nurse's milk was recommended for headaches. Cobwebs placed quickly on a cut finger stopped bleeding.

Children could ward off nightmares by placing their shoes under the bed, soles up. Old people carried a horse chestnut in their pockets as a sure prevention against rheumatism. Some of the old remedies persist today. A few children are still dosed with a spring tonic of bitter dandelion or of sulphur and molasses. Mustard plasters still ease aching joints, and butter and flour take the sting from burns.

Only a rare emergency justified sending for the village doctor, especially if he had to travel by horseback or buggy for miles over country roads. Usually he had little more to offer than the housewife had on hand. He carried in his bag no drugs as we know them today, but only strange concoctions he had pounded and mixed for himself. Dr. Gershom

Bulkely, a famous seventeenth-century physician in Connecticut, left a manual of medicine in which he recorded some of his most effective cures. For a child's "wind colic" he recommended:

> *Take a thick toast of white bread, toasted leisurely to brown. Heat half a pint of muscadine or sack on a pewter dish, very hot, put toast into it. Apply toast to navel as hot as she can endure and let it lie till it be cold.*

Wool, Flax and Spinning Wheels

With so many hours spent over kettle and fire, how could there have been any time left over? Yet in most colonial households every single garment worn by the family had to be made by the women from the raw flax and wool produced on their own land. In addition they wove all the bedding, the window and bed hangings, the rugs, and even the twine. The long process from plant to cloth is unbelievably complicated and wearisome, yet women for thousands of years had taken it for granted, and so did women in America.

Sheep were among the most precious of the creatures imported from England, but the raising of them proved difficult because of wolves. It was many years before wool could be counted upon to supply the clothing needed. The colonists began early to rely on flax. Cotton was not grown until late in the colonial period.

Flax required about twenty different dirty and dusty operations, some so heavy that they were done by the men of the family, before it was ready for spinning. Wool also required many weeks or months of work on its way from the sheep's back to the spinning wheel. One of the most tedious of the processes was the hatcheling which Abigail Foote spoke of in her diary. The fibers of wool or flax were drawn through two hatchels or wire combs till soft fluffy strands were ready for spinning.

The small light spinning wheels which add a quaint decoration to homes and inns today were flax wheels. Wool was spun on a large wheel,

From sheep's back to man's. These panels show the stages of clothmaking from washing the sheep, through shearing, carding, spinning, and weaving.

Left: A reel for winding linen or woolen thread. (Metropolitan Museum of Art)

before which a woman stood, stepping forward and back in rhythm to the quick motion of her arms. Someone has estimated that in the course of a day's spinning a woman walked twenty miles! Spinning was an art that required long practice and a quick and steady hand, and a girl could be proud when she could spin a fine even thread that won her mother's approval.

Even after the spinning, thread was not yet ready for weaving. It had first to be bleached by many soakings, "bucked" in a tub with ashes and hot water, rinsed, beaten and washed repeatedly, and finally spread on the grass to dry in the sun till it acquired a snowy perfection.

"Dyed in the Wool"

The finest thread, which would be woven into a dress or a Sunday coat or a pair of curtains, was dyed a soft color. Every colonial housewife kept handy in a corner a clay dye pot, most often filled with indigo blue, bought from the peddler. Women were also skilled in concocting dyes from the herbs and plants at hand. They made a fine red from dogwood, browns and yellows from sassafras and butternut bark, yellow from onion skins, a gay crimson from the juice of the pokeberry, and a brilliant purple from the paper in which the loaves of imported sugar came wrapped.

Warp and Woof

Carding and spinning were daily, year-round occupations, and women could never afford to have their hands idle for a moment. In early settlements they did their own weaving as well, and long after the Revolution, country women still wove the cloth for the family garments. In many homes the loom was the largest piece of furniture in the kitchen. Made of four heavy beams nearly seven feet high, it took up as much space as a four-poster bed. Later, in prosperous country homes, it was moved into a special weaving room, and in the Southern colonies it occupied a special weaving house.

Threading the loom was a painstaking process requiring two people, for the firm, even texture of the cloth depended on the exact tension of the warp threads. The weaver sat high on a built-up bench at the front of the loom. Weaving was a threefold process. She pressed a foot treadle to raise one of the "heddles" or frames of linen threads, threw the shuttle — containing the woof thread — with one hand, passing it over the flat threads and under the raised threads, and caught it in the other hand, and then slid down a batten bar to push the new thread tightly into place. To weave about three yards of cloth, a good day's work, the weaver had to repeat these three steps three thousand times! Now and again she climbed down from the seat, and wound the new-made length onto

Completing a neighbor's quilt could be a social as well as helpful occasion.

the cloth beam. In the hands of a skillful weaver all this became a rapid and unthinking process, but it required long practice to co-ordinate each step and to gauge the exact motion of the shuttle.

Knowing the time and labor that went into weaving a single piece of cloth, we marvel at a story told by a famous Connecticut preacher. His mother was a widow, who helped her four boys in the field, struggled to nourish them on a diet of corn bread, milk, and bean porridge, and made all their clothing. Once, he recalled, he needed a new suit for some emergency. It was mid-winter and there was no wool left in the house. His mother sheared the half-grown fleece from one of the sheep, carded, spun and wove the wool, and made the suit—all in one week's time! For the rest of the winter the sheared sheep was protected from the cold by a wrapping of braided straw!

A popular homespun material for country people and for children was linsey-woolsey, made of alternating threads of wool and coarse linen. This was cheap, durable, and unbearably scratchy. Just to touch it makes our sympathy go out to little schoolboys clad in linsey-woolsey shirts and trousers, sitting hour after hour on backless benches, their every wriggle bringing a threatening scowl from the schoolmaster. Even more of a torture inflicted on country boys was a practically indestructible home-spun made of the tow which had been combed out of the flax, sometimes reinforced with the bark of prickly wild nettle.

Fancywork

There was so little beauty in the lives of colonial women—perhaps one cherished heirloom, a silver candlestick brought in a trunk from England, a set of gilt buttons, a pair of buckles carefully transferred from the out-worn to the stiff new slippers. The longing for lovely things showed in the pride women brought to their daily work, the scouring to keep the pewter gleaming, the endless bleachings when natural linen would have served

The piecing together of this quilt, begun during the Revolution, was never finished. (New-York Historical Society)

their families just as well, the hot hours over sticky, vile-smelling dye pots to produce a bit of color. And somewhere in their unimaginably busy days, women found time to create pretty things. "Fancywork" has come down to us from the earliest days of the colonies. In later years, when some of the drudgery was lightened, women filled their houses with handiwork. They covered gowns and bed hangings and curtains with incredibly fine embroidery, and trimmed every conceivable object with yards of handmade lace, crocheting and net fringe. The old patterns by which they varied the endless task of weaving have a lovely sound in themselves—"Five Doves in a Row," "All Summer and All Winter," "Pansies in the Wilderness," and "Five Snowballs."

Colonial women also satisfied their longing for beauty by making patchwork quilts. Sometimes these were of wool, warm and enduring. Later, when pretty French calico was fashionable, every scrap was carefully preserved to make quilts of the most elaborate and fanciful patterns. Months of labor went into patching together, with invisible stitches, tiny squares or diamonds. When the patchwork was completed, it was laid on a lining, with layers of wool or cotton between, and fastened to a quilting frame made of four long bars of wood set on chairs. Then came the long-awaited day of the quilting bee. Ten or twelve neighbors were invited, and sitting about the frame they worked together to join the two layers in a close, decorative design of stitching. This part of the quilt-making was never laborious, since it was spiced with gossip and crowned by a feast of cakes and cookies.

Another source of beauty was the flower garden that bloomed by the

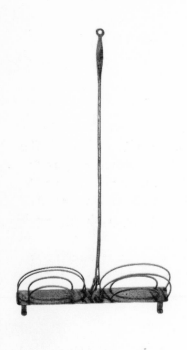

Above: An early toaster. (New-York Historical Society)

Right: Hand-carved herb-crusher, and a wooden pail called a piggin. (Old Sturbridge Village)

doorstep, carefully tended in moments stolen from weeding the corn-patch. The Huguenot women who came from France are said to have brought seeds of hollyhocks and primroses with them in their apron pockets. Dutch women unpacked bulbs of the gay tulips that would transplant a bit of Holland to New Amsterdam. English women soothed their homesickness with the familiar flowers of home—roses and lilies of the valley, foxglove, and Canterbury bells. A frontier bride, riding on a pillion behind her new husband through a frightening wilderness, remembered with comfort the little packet of seeds her mother had tucked in among her household linens.

"To Provide for the Common Defense"

5

Danger was commonplace in the early colonies. There was never a moment in the first settlers' lives when disaster was not close. The awareness of their helplessness in the midst of "a howling wilderness" drew them close together. When Benjamin Franklin told them, in 1776, "We must all hang together, or assuredly we shall all hang separately," they understood him all too well. It had been the principle by which they had lived for one hundred and fifty years.

Starvation, the gravest danger of all in the first year, was soon overcome. The three remaining dangers against which the people banded together were wolves, Indians and fire.

Wolf Hunts

We who have never waked in the night to the cry of wolves cannot imagine the terror this sound brought to the early settlers. At night one could see menacing eyes glowing on the outskirts of a campfire, and even in the daytime shadowy forms haunted the edges of fields. The cry of a pack, which sometimes ran through the forest as many as five hundred strong, must have chilled a settler's blood. Sheep which were desperately needed for food and warm clothing were lost to preying wolves. For economic reasons as well as for safety, the wolves had to be eliminated.

Town meetings voted bounties of eight, ten, or twelve shillings for each wolf head brought to the town treasurer. Besides the reward of shillings, a successful wolf hunter could win fame and glory in his town. In early Puritan settlements he even proudly nailed the bloody wolf heads to the meeting-house door to be admired by passers-by. In Connecticut, General Israel Putnam, who fought bravely in the Revolution, had already made a name for himself in his youth by capturing single-handed a fierce and seemingly unconquerable wolf which had held the whole town in terror. The cave where he made the capture can still be seen, and small boys still crawl into its black depths and shiver at the thought of young Israel venturing in alone with a rope tied about his waist.

Necessity or no, a full-scale wolf hunt was one of the finest sports the colonists enjoyed. An eager crowd of men and boys responded to notices like the following, which appears in the town records of Stratford, Connecticut:

> *It was voted and agreed upon that the next Thursday should be the day to go upon this work of killing wolves ... All persons to be ready by seven of the clock in the morning and meet upon the hill at the meetinghouse by the beat of the drum.*

On such a wolf-rout the men surrounded a section of woods in a wide circle, and moved steadily in, hemming in their prey, as excitement mounted to a high pitch.

Warwhoops and Tomahawks

Two weeks after the landing at Jamestown, Indians made a savage raid on the small settlement. The colony was saved only because the settlers rushed to take shelter in their ships and frightened the Indians by the roar of their cannon. The Pilgrims at Plymouth were also greeted on their arrival by arrows "flying amongst them," with heads made of hart's horn, eagle claws or brass. Until long after the Revolution, every colony was to know at some time the terror of Indian warwhoops.

We should not think, however, that the early settlers lived in daily terror. For long periods Indians and whites dwelled peaceably as neighbors. There were many real friendships between the two races. The Indians taught the white men many things—how to plant corn, how to fish and track game, how to survive in the forest. Powhatan, father of Pocahontas, assured the peace of the Jamestown settlement, and Massasoit was a valuable ally to the Plymouth colony. And a few white men, like John Eliot in Massachusetts, made a sincere effort to establish missions and schools for the Indians.

But conflict was inevitable. To the English, the Indians were an inferior race; some even regarded them as pests to be ruthlessly exterminated. To the Indians, white men were intruders. It didn't matter whether colonists snatched Indian land or paid for it, the Indians never really understood the agreements they signed. When an Indian violated the terms and came back to hunt on his old land, he was hauled into a bewildering English court. The English never understood Indian pride. When an Indian was cheated or insulted, he revenged his injured pride by taking the scalp of some innocent settler working alone in a field. Punishment followed swiftly. Innocent Indians, sometimes a whole village, were deliberately slaughtered as an object lesson. Now and again the smoldering hatred of a tribe would flare into the massacre of a settlement. Several times, under powerful Indian leaders such as King Philip and Pontiac, tribes united for full-scale warfare which was only quelled by the near-extermination of the tribes.

No early settlement dared to go about its business until a fort had been built. Usually this was a palisade of upright logs set close together, with loopholes just big enough to fire a musket through, and a strongly barred gate. At the corners were set the few small cannons from the ships. For the first few years the entire town was enclosed by this fort.

In times of peace the settlers ventured out from the fort and built their cabins and planted their gardens some distance away. But at the first warning of an Indian uprising, families left their homes and fields and moved back inside the fort. Often they had to stay there, crowded into close quarters, for months at a time. In Gorham, Maine, during the Indian raids from 1742 to 1749, the settlers went into the fort and lived there for seven years! When the men went out by day to work the common fields,

NARRATIVE
OF THE
CAPTIVITY, SUFFERINGS AND REMOVES
OF
Mrs. *Mary Rowlandson*,

Who was taken Prisoner by the INDIANS with several others, and treated in the most barbarous and cruel Manner by those vile Savages : With many other remarkable Events during her Travels.

Written by her own Hand, for her private Use, and now made public at the earnest Desire of some Friends, and for the Benefit of the afflicted.

True stories of Indian captivity, like this one of 1773, were very popular in the eighteenth century. (American Antiquarian Society)

Because wolves harassed farm animals, hunting them was both a sport and a necessity.

they posted boys on stumps at the four corners to keep watch while they hoed or harvested.

Indian villages had similar stockades, often ingeniously located in swampy areas and approached by a single narrow bridge. To gain entry into an Indian stockade was no easy task, and in desperation the colonial forces often resorted to the shameful measure of setting fire to the wigwams inside and destroying the village and every inhabitant.

Train Band, Militia, and Continental Army

Except for a few such men as Captain Myles Standish, there were no professional soldiers among the first settlers. In the need for food and shelter no men could be spared from the general labor. Every man had to be both farmer and soldier. In Plymouth each man was required to own a musket, a cartridge belt, a sword, two pounds of powder, and ten pounds of bullets. Churchgoers took their muskets with them and "each sets his arms down near him." Church members took turns keeping watch outside during the long meetings.

Training was needed for farmers and tradesmen who had never before handled a musket, so "train bands" were organized. In 1631 Governor Endicott of Massachusetts issued orders that all planters and servants should be instructed in the use of arms, and that certain days should be set aside for training. The Virginia colonies had a similar law by 1634. Train bands play an important part in the records of every town. Every

Every able-bodied man drilled regularly in training bands on the village green.

able-bodied male between sixteen and sixty was enrolled. No one was exempt.

Training day took place as a rule on one afternoon a month, and absence was punishable by a fine of five shillings. Fines were not often necessary, because training day soon became the chief colonial holiday. Everyone in town turned out to watch the menfolk drill. An account from Judge Sewall's diary gives a good picture of a Boston training day:

> *Eight companies train; many persons; some officers have red paper crosses fastened to their hats. The Governor rode by and among the soldiers ... Gave a volley or two on the common, march'd out about one o'clock to the market place ... Companies gave three volleys, broke off about 3 in the afternoon. In the night a bonfire or two were made on Fort-hill. After followed fire-works with huzzas, ended about 11 or 12.*

After the parade and the required volleys, the men engaged in sports and races. William Byrd was commander in chief of the militia in Virginia

colony, and his diary contains many accounts of "mustering outs." On one day he recorded:

> ... *prepared to go to the general muster of this county ... I found Captain Drury Stith and Captain Eppes there and I caused them to exercise their men till the others came. The first had his troop in good order, but the last had his very indifferent and did not exercise them himself ... about 2 o'clock our prizes began and Will M-rl got the prize of running and John Sc-ls the prize of cudgels and Robin Easely the prize of wrestling.*

Prizes were likely to be guns or swords, and well worth contending for. Judge Sewall once offered a silver cup for the best marksmanship.

The colonial militia, made up of local train bands, was a democratic organization. The colonists had a deep fear of professional soldiers. They put their faith in a citizen army, ready at any moment to take up arms in the public defense. Each town had its independent company and a com-

Left: A Revolutionary drum. Right: A three-cornered cocked hat worn by a captain in 1776. (New-York Historical Society)

mon supply of powder and lead, and each man kept musket and ammunition at home.

When a force was needed to subdue an Indian uprising, a call for volunteers went out. In 1675, when King Philip, sachem of the Wampanoag nation, began his long siege of terror by burning down villages in southern Massachusetts, a call for help went by runners to Boston. Drummers stood on Boston Common and "beat for volunteers," and in three hours one hundred and ten men were mustered.

In the war against the French in Canada, volunteers were recruited from the militia to join the British regulars. In actual fighting they proved that they could more than hold their own, but they found it hard to serve under British command. They resented the rule that even their highest officers were still subordinate to any British officer of the lowest rank. Having learned by tragic experience about Indian warfare, they were infuriated at having to watch the British blundering doggedly ahead with standard tactics that were useless in the forest. They smoldered under the ridicule of British soldiers who strutted in fine scarlet uniforms and drilled with machinelike precision.

From such a situation came one of our most popular songs, "Yankee Doodle." This was a very ancient tune, and was sung by the British soldiers stationed at Albany. They changed the name from "Nankee Doodle," and made up their own words to ridicule the New England militia in their homemade uniforms. Later, British soldiers in Boston used to gather outside the meeting houses and shout the mocking words

Powder flasks and a matchlock musket. (Winchester Gun Museum)

to drown out the psalm-singing. But at the end of the War for Independence, when Cornwallis surrendered to Washington at Yorktown, the Yankee fifers turned the tables and struck up the tune in triumph, and Yankees have sung it with pride ever since.

A large part of the Revolutionary army was recruited from the ranks of the colonial militia. However, it soon was apparent that a regular force would be needed. In 1775 the Continental Congress at Philadelphia voted to raise ten companies of riflemen from Pennsylvania, Maryland and Virginia, to serve for a term of one year. George Washington was made commander in chief of this first army.

The colonial militia had bred many valiant and determined soldiers. At Bunker Hill a troop of untrained, quickly-organized patriots beat back British regulars, who outnumbered them two to one. But General Washington was to find that the militia had many disadvantages. Elected officers changed frequently and were far too indulgent. Training was haphazard and dicipline almost nonexistent. A train band was a local affair, organized for the defense of a community. To save homes and families the men would fight with the last ounce of their strength. But they were not easily persuaded to leave their homes unprotected and march off to a long-drawn out campaign on some distant battlefield. Many of them understood only dimly what the War for Independence was all about. Enlistments were slow, even with special bounties offered as inducement. Men signed up for short periods, usually for three months, and when the term was over they departed for home, even on the day before a major battle. There was a disgraceful record of desertions. Time and again the untrained American forces dissolved and fled before the disciplined British attack, but always they formed again somewhere else. Time and again Washington pleaded with the Congress to pass measures that would assure him a dependable army. But somehow, disorganized and undisciplined as it was, his army held out through sheer stubbornness of spirit until help came from France.

Ragtail Uniforms

Perhaps the well-clad British soldiers had reason to underestimate the patriotism and courage of the American forces. The army often presented as ludicrous an appearance as a train band drilling on a village green. Farmers left their fields and marched off to war in leather breeches and homespun jackets, and their officers, who were usually gentlemen, came in waistcoats and ruffles. There was never a regulation uniform.

To be sure, attempts had been made to outfit the militia, even in the earliest days. Salem in 1628 had ordered twenty full suits of armor. The Connecticut colony in 1650 had purchased fifty "corselets" made of heavy cotton cloth, to be worn over the men's coats as protection against Indian arrows. But armor proved impractical in the wilderness and was discarded along with the old-fashioned long English pikes. Later, prosperous towns voted to equip their own militia with uniforms, each town choosing its own colors. In Connecticut the Governor's Foot Guard wore scarlet coats, bearskin hats, and brown gaiters, exactly as they do today. The City Troops of Philadelphia wore brown coats with white facings, white breeches, high boots and leather caps decorated with bucks' tails. Brown was a favorite color since the dye could be made from plants growing on any farm. Each state added its own colors in hats and trimmings. By Revolutionary times the popular uniform for officers was the buckskin breeches and blue coat with red facings, familiar to us from many colonial paintings. Washington was impressed by the cheap and easy outfits of the frontiersmen—fringed shirt and leggings, with a bag of bullets and a powder horn over one shoulder—and recommended it for the

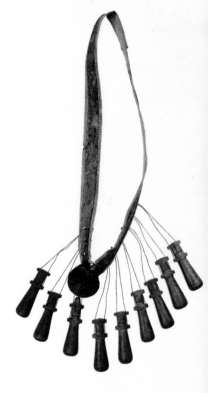

A bandolier, worn over one shoulder. Ammunition powder was kept in the containers. (Winchester Gun Museum)

Continental troops, but as one historian has commented, he never succeeded in securing "any uniform except raggedness."

Throughout the Revolution, though young men were lured into enlisting by promises of handsome uniforms, the army was miserably clothed. Some soldiers even wore red British uniforms bought from privateers or deserters. At one time, when it was impossible to tell the officers from the enlisted men, Washington issued an order that "to prevent mistakes" the commander-in-chief would wear "a light blue ribband across his breast between his coat and his waistcoat." Other officers would be distinguished by pink or green ribbons, or by colored stripes on their sleeves. By the end of the war men sometimes marched with their feet tied in rags.

Flintlock and Rifle

The muskets which the Pilgrims carried to meeting with them were the matchlock or snaphance muskets. To fire them a man had to carry with him a lighted "match" or slow-burning fuse of tow, which had to be carefully protected, fitted into the lock after each loading, and removed and placed at a safe distance before reloading. If he missed the first shot— and these muskets were wildly inaccurate—a deer or rabbit vanished from sight before he could reload. An Indian, instead of vanishing, was more likely to leap at him with a tomahawk. There were seven separate commands for the loading and firing of a matchlock musket, and three volleys on a training day consumed a good part of the drill time.

The flintlock muskets, with which later militia were equipped, did away with the match by using a flint which struck upon a steel plate and produced the spark to ignite the priming powder. Loading a musket was still a complicated procedure. First the exact amount of powder was measured from the powder horn and poured into the barrel. Then the ball was put in, with a small wad of cloth or paper to secure it, and the whole rammed firmly down with the ramrod. The hammer was then set at half cock and the flash pan primed with a finer powder from a second powder horn. The flash pan was closed, the hammer pulled to full cock, and the gun was raised and ready to fire. Incredible as it seems, an experienced soldier could perform this whole operation four times in one minute!

These muskets were considered light, because they could be held breast-high instead of having to rest on a crotched stick. But they weighed well over ten pounds and were five feet long and extremely cumbersome, especially in the forest. They were inaccurate much beyond a range of fifty yards, and there was therefore good reason for the well-known command, "Don't fire until you see the whites of their eyes!" A slight rain or snow made them useless, since the flint would not strike a spark when wet, so a sudden shower could cause a truce in the midst of a battle. Some other annoyances produced two popular expressions which we still use: a "flash in the pan" occurred when the priming powder

Loading a musket.

After training, the men often wrestled for prizes.

caught fire but failed to ignite the charge; to "go off half cocked" was to fire before the hammer was fully cocked.

The frontiersmen brought to the Revolutionary army a far more deadly weapon, the Kentucky rifle, long and light. This had actually been developed in Pennsylvania by the Germans but was adopted by the frontiersmen moving west into Kentucky. Kentucky rifles were flintlock guns, made by hand and often handsomely decorated, no two exactly alike. They were still slow to load, since the ball had to be wrapped in a small "patch" of greased cloth before it was rammed into the barrel. But they were much more accurate than the muskets. In Indian country, where there was seldom chance for a second shot, riflemen developed astonishing markmanship and could hit a small target at a range of 200 yards.

The Roaring Cannon

In the early days of the colonies small cannon imported from England were set up in the forts along the coast and at the mouths of rivers. They were almost impossible to transport by land, and they proved useless in Indian fighting. During the Revolution, when cannon could no longer be imported, colonial foundries learned to cast them of bronze and iron. Washington's army used mobile guns and occasionally larger siege guns. They were drawn by horses or oxen, sometimes taken apart for transportation and then reassembled and maneuvered into position by ropes. The names most commonly mentioned in accounts of battles are culverins, sakers, falcons, howitzers and mortars.

Loading and firing these ancient cannon required a crew of three to seven men, and eight rounds an hour was a good firing rate. Bostonians

The 29th Regiment musters on Boston Common in 1768. (New York Public Library)

evidently found this an entertaining spectacle, for it is said that a crowd used to gather to watch the British soldiers fire their cannon. This was not so hard-hearted as it sounds, for the balls did little damage. In the American forces the men would chase after the rolling balls, pick them up, and remove the fuses. This was risky sport, but for every ball brought to the captain of the regiment a man received a gallon of rum!

Fire!

Not all the danger was from Indians. The first settlers learned very soon that they must unite against another enemy—fire. They sometimes watched the labor of months reduced to ashes or lost a whole family from their small community. The early houses with their log chimneys and thatched roofs were very dangerous. Governor Winthrop in 1630 wrote in his journal:

> *About noon the chimney of Mr. Sharp's house in Boston took fire, the splinters being not clayed at the top, and taking the thatch burnt it down, and the wind being N. W., drove the fire*

to Mr. Colburn's house . . . and burnt that down also, yet they saved most of their goods.

Soon after he recorded:

For the prevention whereof in our new town, intended this summer to be builded, we have ordered that no man there shall build his chimney with wood, nor cover his house with thatch, which was readily assented unto; for that divers other houses have been burned since our arrival.

Every town had laws about fighting fires. In Norwalk, Connecticut, in 1655, every householder was ordered to "set up a good and sufficient ladder reaching up to the chimney above the house." In Boston householders had to have, in addition to the ladder, a long pole with a swab on the end with which to wet the roof. In addition, every family was required to own a leather fire bucket.

In New Amsterdam Governor Peter Stuyvesant summoned a meeting to counsel him about the prevention of fires "which might break out here as well as in other places." As a result, fire wardens were appointed to visit each house. Watchmen patrolled the streets at night, alert to any puff of smoke, armed with a bell to rouse the sleepers. To warn people to be more careful, householders whose houses caught fire were fined, and the fines used for the purchase of more buckets, hooks and ladders. Yet in spite of these precautions, terrible fires broke out. In Boston in 1673 forty-six houses and a meeting house burned to the ground because one boy fell asleep and left his candle burning.

Bucket Brigades and Rival Pumpers

At an alarm every citizen instantly responded. Church bells tolled, and everyone in town rushed to help. If a citizen could not go at once, he

A prominent citizen, said to be George Washington, joins in fire-fighting practice. (Historical Collection of Insurance Company of North America)

flung his fire bucket into the street, so that the first passer-by could snatch it up. Sometimes four men would run through the streets to collect buckets, with long poles on their shoulders on which they could string twenty-four buckets at a time.

Quickly a double line of men and boys, and often women and girls too, would form from the blazing house to the nearest pond or stream. A steady relay of buckets passed from hand to hand. As soon as the contents were splashed on the flames, the empty bucket went back down the other line. The men at the head of the line needed courage, for they had to stand very close to the scorching heat in order to hurl the slight contents of a bucket onto the flames. Fast as the men worked, they could seldom win against the enemy, but they could sometimes save the neighboring houses by drenching the roofs. When the house was reduced to ruins the men collected their buckets and went home.

Boston imported its first fire engine from England in 1659. It was a crude wooden cart drawn by hand, with a small tank and a syringe which squirted water on the flames. It took three or four men to manage the pump handle, and they worked so hard that sometimes they had to be relieved every two minutes. The engine did not do away with the bucket brigade. Water to fill the tank still had to pass from hand to hand, but the stream from the syringe, inaccurate and feeble, reached higher than a man could throw. By 1725 new fire engines from England could project a continuous stream.

Along with the fire engines came the fire brigades. These volunteer companies, which still exist in American towns, are a lively proof of the American spirit of "all for one." The first volunteer fire company was formed in Philadelphia under the advice of Benjamin Franklin. The men called their company "The Union," and later Franklin himself served as their chief. Similar fire brigades were soon organized throughout the colonies. Besides the engine, and the hooks and ladders, each member carried two canvas bags for salvaging articles from burning houses, and a bed key for taking bedsteads apart.

As soon as a town purchased a second fire engine, a second fire brigade was organized, and a fierce rivalry sprang up between the two companies. The men made extravagant boasts about their own engines, and gave them names such as Honey Bee, Hayseed, Damper or Deluge. After a fire they would embrace their engines and decorate them with emblems. At first these fire companies operated as insurance companies. Subscribers were given metal badges to display on their houses, and if a fire company arrived at a burning house and found a rival badge they would not even try to put out the blaze. Presently common sense did away with this practice, and companies united to fight every fire.

In larger towns four or five engines with their companies would rush into a battle that was both a marvel of teamwork and a bitter competition. They would take stands the length of a hose apart, like the old bucket

A leather fire bucket. (Old Sturbridge Village)

A bucket brigade in action illustrates the announcement of a meeting of the Hand-in-Hand Fire Company. (New York Public Library)

An old print showing volunteers fetching water and manning a pumper.
(New-York Historical Society)

brigades, between the burning house and the pond, pumping water from
one engine to the next till the last hose reached the flames. By pumping
furiously the men of one company could sometimes "wash" the next
engine; that is, they could pump the water in so fast that the men
pumping on the next engine could not empty it out before the tank overflowed. This was such a disgrace that men would pump themselves
breathless to defend the honor of their engine, and if it was washed,
exhausted men often wept with shame. This battle of the engines was
frequently better sport for the spectators than was the fire itself.

A visitor from France, Morceau de St. Mery, wrote:

> *The zeal and eagerness with which all Americans fight fires*
> *are admirable, but at the same time there are so many willing*
> *helpers and there is so little order that they do more harm*
> *than good . . . in general the workers have too good a time.*

In spite of the uproar and excitement, the fire brigades fought a brave
battle against the ancient enemy. In 1781 Benjamin Franklin was able to
report that "the city has never lost by fire more than one or two houses at
a time, and the flames have often been extinguished before the house in
which they began has been half consumed."

School Days

6

In the spring of 1802, a fourteen-year-old boy with the dignified name of Theophilus Sargent journeyed with his father north from Massachusetts far into the Maine forest. Together they felled trees, made a small clearing, built a two-room cabin, and planted a corn patch. Then the father returned to Massachusetts for the rest of his family, leaving his son to tend the crop. Illness delayed the family for many months, and the river was beginning to freeze over when they finally reached their new home. All this time Theophilus stayed alone in the wilderness. When his last food was stolen by a marauding bear, he might have perished if a wandering tribe of Indians had not befriended him.

Pioneer boys and girls were frequently called upon to do man-sized jobs. A boy learned to handle a gun almost as soon as he could hold it. One of the largest wolves ever killed in Pennsylvania was shot by a ten-year-old boy. Girls did not often learn to shoot, but sometimes they had to use their wits instead. A girl in Maine, alone in a cabin, once saw a huge bear in the garden patch. She quickly filled an earthenware dish with a mixture of rum and molasses and set it outside the door. The bear lapped it up greedily and promptly lay down to sleep off the effects. The grandmother, returning home from a neighbor's, helped the girl to chain the sleeping bear to a stump, and there he waited to surprise the menfolk when they came home from hunting.

Childhood was never a carefree time in the early colonies. Families lived close together, crowded into small cabins, sharing whatever came from day to day. Death was a familiar visitor in every household, and children could not be shielded from the ugly and frightening aspects of life. They had very little time to play. They were expected to work hard, to study their lessons and their catechisms, to be obedient and respectful. They addressed their parents as "honored sir," or "esteemed parent," and did not speak without permission. Their parents believed wholeheartedly in the proverb, "Spare the rod and spoil the child." Often the survival of the whole family depended on rigid discipline. At the first warning of an Indian attack children knew they must obey instantly without question, and even the littlest learned to lie in hiding without a whimper. Such children grew up early. At sixteen a boy was a man and could vote and bear arms, and at the same age a girl often went as a bride into her own home.

The Shadow of Doomsday

Without a doubt Puritan children in New England had the hardest time of all. More than they feared Indians or starvation, Puritan parents feared

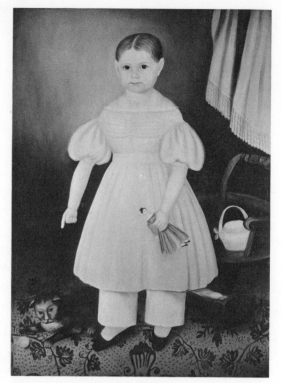

sin, and they thought it their duty to impress this fear on their children. There is a story told of Judge Samuel Sewall of Boston that one day, finding his rainspout out of order, he discovered a ball belonging to one of his children lodged in it. He sent for the minister, and they held a long session of prayer with the boy, explaining to him that he must constantly fight against the powers of darkness that tempted him to such mischief!

Three-year-olds were required to memorize the Young Child's Catechism, which contained such warnings as:

> Question: *What must become of you if you are wicked?*
> Answer: *I shall be sent down to everlasting Fire and Hell among wicked and miserable creatures.*

On Sabbath mornings boys and girls with some slight mischief on their consciences must have sat shivering as the preacher described in terrifying detail the tortures that awaited sinners.

For almost a century after the worthy Puritan fathers had ceased to rule New England, their influence cast a heavy shadow over children. The New England Primer, which was the most popular reading book for children until long after the Revolution, taught the alphabet by such verses as:

> *As runs the Glass*
> *Our life doth pass.*
>
> *While Youth do cheer*
> *Death may be near.*

William Howard Smith was only five and his sister Mary Jane was only two when these portraits were made, but the artist has painted them as small adults. (Abby Aldrich Rockefeller Folk Art Collection)

Every girl displayed her mastery of embroidery by working moral lessons into a "sampler." (New-York Historical Society)

ABCDEFGHIKLMNOP RSTUVWXYZ . 123456789

nted
Conted with my   Seek to be good
humble State   Instead of grate
I will Pass my   And Sing my
peacefull days   makers prase

In thy
Youth
Fear the
God of
Truth

wouldst thou live long keep
time in high esteem
when gone if thou canst
not recall redeem

if all Mankind Would live in mutual Love
This World would much resemble that above

Mary
Halls Work
In The 12 yea
of her age
1800

The first little books printed and sold just for children were never intended for their amusement alone, but always for their moral instruction. The earliest ones were stories of pious children who died at an early age, or of naughty children who came to a sorry end. Even little tales which promised to be about games or sports taught a moral lesson. A good example is a long poem (quoted by Monica Kiefer in *American Children Through Their Books*) about a little boy named Harry who went fishing:

> *Many a little fish he caught*
> *And pleased was he to look*
> *To see them writhe in agony*
> *And struggle on the hook.*

The poem goes on to describe Harry as he proudly carried home his catch and met the just reward of his cruelty:

> *But as he climbed to reach a dish*
> *To put his fishes in*
> *A large meat hook that hung close by*
> *Did catch him by the chin.*
>
> *Poor Harry kicked and called aloud*
> *And screamed and cried and roared,*
> *While from his wounds the crimson blood*
> *In dreadful torrents pour'd.*

Yet we know from early letters and diaries that Puritan parents loved and enjoyed their children in spite of their sternness. Even Judge Sewall, like any devoted father, recorded in his diary such world-shaking events as the first word spoken by the new baby. It was said of Cotton Mather, the great preacher who held his listeners spellbound with fear, that he used to entertain his children with delightful stories every day, and that the "sorest punishment" he could inflict was to send a child out of his presence for a while. One Puritan father made for his little son a set of blocks to teach him his letters. The clumsy little wooden toys which have been preserved for three hundred years are the best evidence of all, for they speak plainly of moments stolen from the endless round of work to fashion with care a little jointed doll or a horse and wagon for some loved child.

Chores from Dawn to Dark

As early settlements grew into towns with rows of comfortable houses, life for children became less terrifying. But there was still plenty of work to be done. Boys and girls shared the work of the household, sowing and weeding, hoeing corn, making brooms, scouring and scrubbing. Henry Ward Beecher, the famous preacher, though he lived some time after colonial days were past, left us a fine account of a typical country boy-

A primer lesson on parchment covered by a sheet of horn, as in this 18th-century example, was called a hornbook. (Colonial Williamsburg)

A Dame School. Holding their hornbooks, children gather in a neighbor's kitchen to learn their ABC's.

hood. He rose long before dawn and built the kitchen fire in the dark, before morning prayers, with wood that he had chopped in the summer months. In the winter he sometimes had to shovel a tunnel in the snow to reach the woodpile. He cared for the horses and cows. When the water froze in the well he drove the oxen two miles to the river, broke the ice, and filled barrels with water for washday. All this before setting off for a long day at school. In the evenings he hemmed towels and knit suspenders and mittens, and would have been surprised to hear that only girls did such tasks.

In the same spirit little girls helped their brothers in the fields. But they were adept at household tasks, having helped their mothers from the time they could walk. Many of the complicated steps in cloth-making were done entirely by children, who hatcheled the flax, combed wool, wound spools, and very early learned to spin. It was said that a girl should be able to piece a quilt by the time she was three. Girls of six or seven knit stockings—one Vermont family remembered that a customary stint was fifteen times around a stocking before breakfast—and wove their own shoelaces and belts and ribbons on small tape-looms. One little girl in Shelburne, New Hampshire, knit the alphabet and a verse of poetry into a single pair of mittens! The bits of "fancywork" done by children of that day astonish us. Occasionally, sad to say, a stint of fine embroidery was assigned as a punishment.

Every little girl had her sampler. Originally these embroidered pictures were intended as practice for the tiny uniform stitches a girl must learn to make. Once finished they were a sort of diploma, hung on the wall with pride. We cannot look at a sampler today without pity for the rebellious small fingers cramped for endless hours over a needle. But for many girls a sampler was a labor of love, into which she wove all her imagination and her love of pretty things. These incredibly intricate and perfect little embroidered squares, some still bright and unfaded today, are preserved in museums and historical societies. We marvel at the exact rows of lettering—the alphabet, Bible verses, whole stanzas of poetry—the scrolls of flowers, and the quaint, flat little houses and animals and people. A sampler was truly a diploma, testifying that a girl had learned patience and painstaking skill.

Dolls, Kites and Jackknives

Only when the chores were done was there time for play. Colonial children had few real toys, and most of these were homemade. Little girls must always have had dolls of some sort, even in the earliest and hardest days. They were carved from wood by patient fathers and brothers, and sometimes they even had jointed arms and legs. There were corncob dolls, and braided cornhusk dolls with their silky hair, and rag dolls with indigo-painted eyes and berry-red mouths. In a wealthy city home one of the valuable fashion dolls imported from France might, when her gown was no longer in style, find its way into a little girl's possession, but only for looking at, not for loving. Indulgent fathers and grandfathers made doll-sized cradles and chairs. Occasionally a fortunate child possessed a tiny set of dishes, pewter or china, imported from England. For the most part, dolls ate from leaf dishes and drank from acorn cups. "In those early times," wrote Harriet Beecher Stowe, "the life of childhood was much more in the imagination than now."

Above: Country fathers often whittled toys for their children. (Old Sturbridge Village)

Right: An 18th-century wooden doll. (Colonial Williamsburg)

A child's rocking horse. (New-York Historical Society)

By the middle of the eighteenth century there were toymakers in the large cities, but their products seldom reached country children. Spinning tops and marbles were advertised in Boston before the Revolution. On Boston Common the boys rolled hoops made from sea-going barrels, and on spring days the sky over Park Street was alive with kites. Country boys made balls from old stocking ravelings covered tightly with sheepskin. A favorite Dutch toy was knucklebones, a game similar to jackstones and played with sheeps' knuckles.

Every boy had one favorite possession, which was both a toy and a necessity—his jackknife. With it he could construct his own playthings, whistles from willow sticks, tops, bows and arrows, and any number of inventions.

Parties and Pets

Everywhere, in all the colonies, children played the same games of hide-and-seek, blindman's buff, tag, which seem to spring up, with different names and variations, in every land and time, wherever there are children. Parties in the city were likely to be smaller editions of grown-up parties, where sashed and beruffled little girls and velvet-clad little boys minced through the steps of the minuet in imitation of their elders. Country parties were more boisterous affairs, with lively games and picnics.

One young lady who visited the Dutch settlement at Albany left in her diary an account of a custom which will have a familiar sound to many children today:

> *The Saturday before Easter every family boils a basket of eggs, colouring them in a curious manner. They are boiled very hard, and each of the family takes several, goes among his intimates, challenging them to butts. The eggs are struck together, and the one that is broken given to the one who breaks it. There is much merriment in it . . .*

Country children had their dog and cat playmates and also made pets of young deer, beavers, squirrels and wild geese. Raccoons made especially

An etching by a famous American painter, Charles Wilson Peale, shows chimney sweeps laughing at a little girl who has dropped her pie. (Library of Congress)

fine companions, easy to tame, but they could never be cured of stealing, and they had an irresistible fondness for sweets. Imagine a mother's horror at the sight of a little black paw in that precious china bowl of sugar lumps hoarded for a tea party!

The English visitor, Mary Russell, in 1796, purchased a mockingbird in New Jersey for eleven dollars, "a very fine bird and a good singer." And in New York she bought "six little yellow birds in a cage."

Fashions for Little Adults

During most of the colonial period children dressed like little models of their elders. No one thought of designing clothes especially for children's active bodies. Babies, of course, both boys and girls, wore long dresses and petticoats, and they remained babies for a long time. Portraits of little boys, three and four years old and even older, show them in long dresses much like those their mothers were wearing, with heavy hanging sleeves and stiff yokes. We hope these were only for state occasions such as having portraits painted.

When they graduated from baby clothes, children donned the same styles as their elders. Boys went into tight knee breeches and waistcoats, girls into voluminous petticoats, tight bodices and caps. Little girls of three and four sometimes wore corsets from underarm to knee, made of strips of steel or whalebone tightly stitched into heavy canvas, in order to improve their posture. Young gentlemen, both in Virginia and in northern cities, wore wigs at the age of eight or nine.

An order which George Washington sent to England for clothes for his little stepdaughter mentioned such items as a coat of fashionable silk, a satin hat, twelve pairs of mitts and six pairs of white kid gloves.

Such exaggerated fashions were of course only found in cities and in wealthy homes. Country boys and girls, in their simple homespun clothes of linsey-woolsey, were far more carefree. While the Southern miss wore gloves and a linen mask to protect her delicate skin, country children used sunbonnets which they helped to make by pasting old newspapers together to form a limp cardboard which was then covered with scraps of gaily printed calico.

The Three R's

As soon as the colonists had made certain of shelter and a place for worship they turned their attention to schooling. Education for their children was an essential part of their dream, and each settlement set about it by one method or another. In the South and in the Middle Colonies education remained for a long time an individual matter, left to parents and to private schools. It was in the closely settled towns of New England that public education as we know it had its beginning, and the story of our first schools is a New England story. However, though these early schools were supported by the towns, they were far from democratic. When laws were passed regarding schooling for children, the word "children" meant only boys. Girls were universally excluded from all town schools until long after the Revolution. And the schools actually included only boys who seriously intended to prepare for college, since the rigid course of study soon discouraged all others.

The first schools, called grammar schools, did not, like our grammar schools today, give elementary training. It was taken for granted that a boy could read when he entered, even though many boys entered grammar school at the age of seven. Ambitious parents taught their children to read when they were two or three years old. Timothy Dwight, one day to be president of Yale College, could read the Bible before he was four. Many small boys learned to read Latin as well; Jonathan Edwards, later a famous preacher, mastered Latin grammar before he was seven. A letter from his father, who had interrupted the teaching of his son to serve in the militia, reminded his mother to make sure that young Jonathan said over what he had learned each day, and that he teach his younger sisters whatever he had learned.

A kind brother and a bad boy. (Free Library of Philadelphia)

Boys who did not learn to read at home attended a dame school. This was a small private school, somewhat similar to our kindergarten, run by a woman who taught perhaps eight or ten pupils in her own kitchen. She not only prepared small boys for the grammar school, but she also took in little girls and gave them the only formal learning that most of them would ever have. A woman did not need much education to qualify as mistress of a dame school. She needed only to teach her young charges their letters, perhaps the simplest addition and subtraction, to knit and sew, and to mind their manners.

The children learned their ABC's from a hornbook. This was not really a book at all, but a single piece of paper sometimes only three by four inches, fastened to a small wooden paddle. A good deal of material was crowded onto this one small sheet of paper. There was the alphabet, both large and small letters, and a series of combinations such as ab, eb, ib; ac, ec, ic. These were followed by a benediction and often by the Lord's Prayer. The name hornbook came from the thin sheet of transparent horn which protected the printed paper, and which was fastened down with a narrow strip of brass and small nails. Sometimes the handle of the paddle was pierced with a hole and a string attached so that a child could wear his book about his neck.

In the Dutch colonies an ingenious manufacturer invented cooky molds of heavy wood in the shape of hornbooks, and these gave small pupils an added incentive for learning their letters, since the book itself was their reward. In wealthy city homes a rare gift to a pampered daughter was a dainty hornbook of carved ivory or silver. Later, as printing presses became more numerous, hornbooks were succeeded by small folded cards known as battledores, which contained little pictures as well as the alphabet. They sold for a penny apiece and were enormously popular.

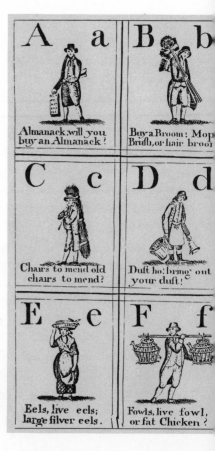

Once a child mastered his hornbook, he graduated to the New England Primer. This version of the English primers was being printed in Boston by 1690. Reprinted and revised, over and over, it found its way into every colonial home and school. Young and old learned from it, for it not only served as a first reader, but little verses such as "In Adam's fall, We sinned all," taught Puritan doctrines in a simple way that everyone could understand. Besides the alphabet verses, the primer contained the Lord's Prayer and the Creed, some religious verses and precepts, and the Shorter Catechism. The tiny engravings that enlivened the pages were surprisingly clear and full of detail. One illustration which every child must have remembered all his life was the picture of John Rogers, a Protestant martyr, burning at the stake, surrounded by his wife and ten children. The picture was accompanied by a long poem which he wrote to his children before his death.

From the New England Primer a child went directly to the Bible. After all, to read the Bible was the main purpose in learning to read at all, and for most children the goal was reached when they could spell out the sacred words. Serious scholars were ready now for Latin.

The shock to a small boy of seven or eight when he left the kindly

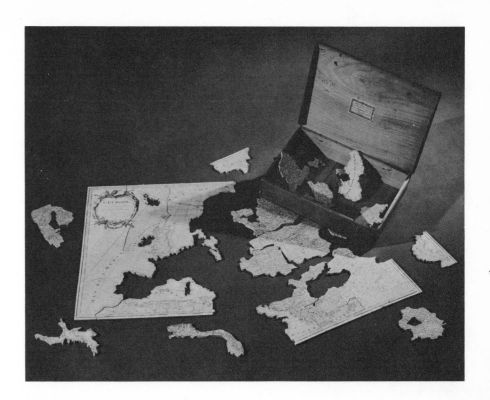

A wealthy Virginian imported this French jigsaw puzzle of the map of Europe. (Colonial Williamsburg)

Street scenes are used to teach the alphabet on this lesson card. (Free Library of Philadelphia)

dame school kitchen and entered the grammar school must have been so cruel that it is no wonder many boys abandoned their education then and there. The small bleak schoolhouse was freezing in winter, the benches narrow and backless, the hours long, the studies monotonous, and the discipline rigid.

The sole aim of the grammar school was to prepare boys for college, and the requirements of Harvard College, the first college established in the colonies, give a good idea of the course of study a boy needed to pursue.

> *Whoever shall be able to read Tully, or any such-like classical author at sight, and correctly, without assistance to speak and write Latin both in prose and verse, and to inflect exactly the paradigms of Greek nouns and verbs, has a right to expect to be admitted into the college, and no one may claim admission without these qualifications.*

To meet these requirements a boy set himself to master a Latin grammar, and a drearier, more discouraging textbook never confronted any scholar. Josiah Quincy, who was mayor of Boston and President of Harvard College, left in his autobiography a vivid picture of his first days at school:

> *The truth was, I was an incorrigible lover of sports of every kind. My heart was in ball and marbles, I needed and loved perpetual action of body ... I was compelled to sit with four other boys on the same hard bench daily, four hours in the morning and four in the afternoon, and study lessons which I could not understand ... the rule being that there should be*

no advance until the first book was conquered, I kept in Cheever's Accidence I know not how long. All I know is, I must have gone over it twenty times before mastering it.

He was six years old!

Arithmetic was no better. Today the ancient textbooks seem almost incomprehensible, yet boys were expected to make their own way, memorizing rules and laboring over sums, with no assistance. John Trumbull, a Connecticut lawyer, recalled that at the age of twelve he had read Virgil, Cicero, Horace and many other authors in Latin, and the Greek testament and Homer's *Iliad* in Greek. But in arithmetic he met "an awful stumbling block." He was once stumped by a problem with which he struggled for three months, his master having forbidden anyone to help him, till suddenly, in a flash, the solution came to him.

Boys who sat at backless benches for eight hours a day were kept at their labors by a relentless schoolmaster. The slightest disorder was quelled by stinging blows from a birch rod. If a boy failed to recite correctly, he was either lazy or stupid, and the same punishment was the cure for both. Masters also devised ingenious and humiliating punishments such as pinching a boy's nose in a split stick, or forcing him to balance for long periods on a one-legged stool. Parents approved this discipline; they felt that a schoolboy who wasn't frequently whipped must not be learning much. At no time did it ever seem to occur to anyone that learning might be fun.

Perhaps the master himself deserves a word of pity. His life was not an easy one. To qualify as schoolmaster a young man needed a stout heart more than vast learning. His wages were low and uncertain, paid in corn, turnips, onions, firewood or other produce. Though his desk was nearest the fire, the green wood with which parents paid their sons' tuitions did not always give off enough heat to thaw the ink frozen in the inkpot. He had to keep control all day of an explosive roomful of boys who were likely to retaliate by such tricks as stuffing the chimney and smoking him out. He was shifted about to board for so many weeks at a time with one grudging parent after another. And he must spend his evenings setting out the lines to be copied next morning. Yet there were gifted teachers who ruled their classes with gentleness and earned the undying loyalty of their boys.

After the middle of the eigtheenth century the church began to lose its strong influence and people were more interested in "getting ahead" than in schooling. Parents who desired a good education for their boys sent them to a new type of school, the private academy. Although Latin and Greek were still the major studies, academies introduced new subjects and more activities for students, including debates, plays, even athletic contests.

One important innovation was the weekly speaking of pieces, when each boy recited before the whole school some bit of prose or poetry that he had memorized. Edward Everett Hale, a famous preacher, once said that he owed to this early training his ease in speaking in public. But

MR. JOHN ROGERS, minister of the gospel in *London*, was the first martyr in Queen MARY's reign, and was burnt at *Smithfield, February* 14, 1554.—His wife with nine small children, and one at her breast following him to the stake; with which sorrowful sight he was not in the least daunted, but with wonderful patience died courageously for the gospel of JESUS CHRIST.

This picture of John Rogers being burned at the stake was a familiar part of the New England Primer. (Free Library of Philadelphia)

Daniel Webster, one of America's outstanding orators, had a different recollection of his years in an academy. He later wrote in his autobiography:

> *I believe I made tolerable progress in most branches ... but there was one thing I could not do. I could not make a declamation. I could not speak before the school ... Many a piece did I commit to memory, and recite and rehearse, in my own room, over and over again; yet when the day came, when the school collected to hear declamations, when my name was called, and I saw all eyes turned to my seat, I could not raise myself from it ... When the occasion was over, I went home and wept bitter tears of mortification.*

College for the Chosen Few

College, for the few boys who finally achieved it, was just more of the same Spartan course of study. Life at Harvard, Yale, Dartmouth, Princeton, or any early college, was hard and uncomfortable. Rooms were meagerly heated with open fireplaces, meals were skimpy, hours were long—from six in the morning till dinner time, with enforced study in the evening, and only one hour after the evening meal for relaxation. Rules of conduct were rigid, and offenses such as card-playing, frequent-

A one-room schoolhouse. As punishment, the boy in front is being made to wear a wooden gag and sign.

ing a public tavern, disrespect to masters, even shouting and "jostling," were subject to fines or public punishment.

Yet college boys, not so different from those today, still found ways to amuse themselves. One Harvard graduate remembered the cannonballs which every boy kept in his room to heat at the hearth for bedwarmers, and which could also be rolled downstairs "at such time as might most nearly bisect a proctor's night-sleep." A Yale graduate recalled the "Christmas procession" when the boys marched about New Haven with horns, pans, pails and clubs, arousing sleeping citizens. There was also a time-honored Yale ceremony of burying Euclid, the geometry textbook, with great pomp at the end of the course. Before the funeral, a red-hot poker was driven through the book so that for once the boys could see through it!

Little Red Schoolhouse

The vast majority of colonists did not expect their sons to go to college. They did want them to have basic training in the three R's, and this need was finally met by the district schools which were built in every small town near the end of the eighteenth century. A small town district might have only ten dollars a year for its school, and could only afford a winter term of ten or twelve weeks and perhaps a summer term for younger pupils.

No matter how many pupils or how varied their ages, one room and one teacher had to suffice. Older pupils worked at benches drawn up ... a shelf built alo... ...ing in their books the

Yale College students sometimes forgot to be sober and studious.

lessons which the schoolmaster had set out for them. The younger pupils sat on lower benches in the middle of the room, the smallest with their feet dangling, and waited patiently for their turn to recite. There was seldom more than one primer or arithmetic, which never left the master's hand. Spelling lessons were learned by the whole school at once, each word repeated after the master, so loudly that in summer their voices could be heard for a long distance across the fields.

Equipment was almost entirely homemade. Pupils made at home their own copybooks by stitching together sheets of heavy brown paper and covering them with cardboard or wallpaper. They ruled the sheets with plummets made by melting down lead and running it into a crack in the floor to form a little tomahawk-shaped wedge which they tied to their rulers. Although lead pencils were sold in Boston as early as 1740, most country boys had never seen one even a hundred years later. They copied their lines and worked their sums in ink which they made at home by boiling down the bark of swamp maple in water to a thick dark syrup. Their pens were goose quills, and the shaping of them required real skill and was usually done by the schoolmaster himself. Slates did not come into use until 1820. A well-equipped school might boast a wooden globe of the world. There were no blackboards, no pictures, nothing colorful or bright anywhere to relieve the drab board walls.

But there was Exhibition Day, the crowning day of the school year. On this day parents and townsfolk crowded into the schoolroom. Months of preparation went into the specimens of clear, uniform handwriting which were passed from hand to hand. Many of these beautiful exhibition pieces have been preserved for us, and though they seem a waste of valuable time, they did testify that the young scholars had acquired patience, exactness, and self-control, all qualities which would serve them well in life.

An exciting feature of these Exhibition Days was the spelling bee,

With colours flying, drum and fife,
They mimic Soldiers to the life.

Who ever play'd at Blindman's-Buf
And was the first to cry "Enough?"

Children at play. (Free Library of Philadelphia)

a contest filled with almost unbearable suspense. The moment when a scholar stood alone, the victor of the spelling bee, might be the only taste of fame he would ever know, and the memory of the applause of his admiring audience might linger even in his old age.

"A tender and interesting branch"

What of the girls, whom we have scarcely mentioned? A resolution passed in Gloucester, Massachusetts, in 1790 contained a surprising provision—two hours at the time of day most convenient for the school should be devoted to the instruction of females, "as they are a tender and interesting branch of the Community, but have been much neglected in the Public schools of this town." Girls had, indeed, been much neglected everywhere. At the time of the Revolution the wives of many of the leading patriots could not read. Many ancient wills are signed with the simple "x" that shows that a woman could not even write her own name. Colonial men believed that too much reading addled a woman's brain and might even be dangerous to her sanity.

A few privileged girls, like the sisters of Jonathan Edwards, learned Latin, and wealthy families sometimes engaged tutors for their daughters as well as their sons. For the most part, singing, playing on a musical instrument, and manners were considered the essentials of a genteel education. Dancing was an important accomplishment, and so was dainty needlework.

Girls everywhere, rich and poor, at last found opportunity in the district schools, but this came about very gradually. Sometimes they were allowed to come for two hours late in the afternoon after the boys had been released, and sometimes they had an early session from five to seven in the morning. It was long after 1800 before girls attended the schools on equal terms with their brothers.

Family Portrait

Perhaps we have painted too dark a picture of colonial childhood. There were bright and happy moments too, and of all these perhaps the times

Do not at See-Saw be found.
Lest you see-saw it on the ground.

This healthy exercise and play
Suits best upon a frosty day.

grown-up children remembered best were the long winter evenings around the kitchen fireplace. The leaping flames in the hearth drew the family into a snug circle of warmth and light. This was a time of contentment, but not of idleness. The women and girls kept their fingers busy with the sewing and knitting and spinning that was never done. Children scraped kernels of corn from the dried cobs or knit socks and mittens for the snowy days ahead.

While the others worked, an older child might read aloud familiar stories from the Bible or even a sermon. Perhaps mothers and fathers repeated the old folk tales and legends they had heard as children—Jack and the Beanstalk or Tom Thumb. Or Grandfather willingly told again the story of how he had crawled into the deep cave to capture the king of the wolves, and how the fearsome brute had rolled over like a puppy to have his stomach tickled. Or Grandmother knotted a bit of linen thread and made a cat's cradle. There would be a treat of roasted apples or popcorn and cider, and the children would beg for one more story before they scurried off to their icy beds upstairs. These were the memories that later might warm a homesick bride in a frontier cabin, or a young soldier, frozen and ragged, camping with General Washington's army. Perhaps they more than made up for the dangers and the hardships.

Tradesmen and Craftsmen

7

The first settlements in America were financed by companies in England which chartered ships for the voyage and provided food, tools and weapons for a beginning in the New World. To transport a man from England to America cost about ten pounds, and in addition he had to be supported until he could raise a crop. The cost of establishing a family in a new colony was, in today's values, several thousands of dollars. The first obligation of the settlers was to find a way to repay this debt. Of necessity almost all colonists became farmers, raising the food and clothing needed for their own families. In addition, in each section of the country, they set to work to discover the natural products that could be sent back to England. By the time the debt was repaid, each colony had developed its own basis for a thriving trade.

In Virginia, Maryland and North Carolina, tobacco proved to be most profitable. In South Carolina and Georgia the leading product was rice. These crops were grown mainly on large plantations with slave labor, but small independent farms also contributed a share.

The Middle Colonies were known as the "bread colonies." From New York and Pennsylvania farms, with their rich soil, quantities of grain, beer, beef and pork were exported to England and the West Indies. From these colonies also went huge shipments of furs obtained through trade with the Indians and collected at the trading center in Albany.

New Englanders, managing a bare living from the stony soil, had to find other means of making a profit. Except for lumber there were few natural resources. From the beginning New England turned to the sea to make a living in shipbuilding, fishing and trade.

Shallop and Schooner

Since the only way for the first colonists to get about was by water, they were soon constructing small shallops—open boats with both oars and sails—suitable for fishing along the coast and for traveling on the rivers. Among the settlers at Plymouth was an English ship carpenter, and six shipwrights arrived at Salem, bringing with them the necessary pitch, tar, cordage and sailcloth. Fine oak lumber was everywhere at hand. Soon American-made boats were sailing all along the coast, from Maine to Virginia. Fishing boats were mainly simple, round-bottomed boats with a single mast and a square sail, with a small triangular sail near the stern. A Gloucester shipbuilder, Captain Andrew Robinson, rigged his ketch with two masts, fore and aft sails, and a jibsail. His ship scudded along at such a pace that onlookers said it "schooned"—the word for

Fishing, especially for cod and mackerel, was a major industry in New England.

a stone skipping the water — and all ships rigged in this way were called schooners. There were also small boats known as pinks, snows and cheboccos.

The first large vessel was the *Onrust,* built in New Amsterdam in 1616. The first English sloop capable of ocean travel was *The Blessing of the Bay,* built in Medford, Massachusetts. This sloop began a lively trade with the Dutch at New Amsterdam. Ten years later a "great ship" of 300 tons, larger than almost any ships then sailing the ocean, was launched at Salem. So began an important industry.

In 1661 England, attempting to shut out American trade with other countries, passed the Navigation Act, which ordered that all American exports must be carried in English-built ships. Since the colonists interpreted English-built as also meaning American-built, this act, which was intended to curb the growing colonial trade, acted as a spur to the ship-building industry. Shipyards sprang up all along the coast. By 1665 there were 300 New England ships on the seas. By 1720 Boston shipyards alone were producing 200 ships a year, and Philadelphia was rapidly becoming a rival. Since it cost only half as much to build ships in America because of the abundant supply of lumber, English merchants purchased many of the ships launched from American shipyards.

The Sacred Cod

No wonder a model of a codfish hangs in the State House in Boston! This lowly fish, which had been the main support of the Pilgrims, soon

Philadelphia shipyard craftsmen hard at work on a man-of-war.
(Library of Congress)

Arch Street Ferry, Philadelphia, from an engraving. (Library of Congress)

provided a livelihood for hundreds of New Englanders and eventually brought fortunes to many a Massachusetts merchant. Salted, dried, and packed in barrels, it was shipped out in great quantities. Fleets of small homemade sloops went out in increasing numbers from Salem and Marblehead and Gloucester, and from the small settlements along the coast of Maine. Soon they were casting their lines as far north as the Grand Banks of Newfoundland.

New England fishermen were independent, weather-toughened men, who endured incredible hardships. In addition to the cold and wind and constant danger, the daily labor was severe. All fishing was done by lines lowered from the deck, and fish weighing more than forty pounds were pulled up hand over hand. When a school of fish followed the ship the men could not rest for an instant from this backbreaking labor.

There She Blows!

The most adventurous of all the hardy race of fishermen were those who followed the great whales. Indians and white settlers sometimes caught

Codfish drying on racks in Provincetown, from an old engraving.
(New-York Historical Society)

whales not far from the New England shores. But soon after 1700, sailors from Nantucket captured a new kind of whale, the sperm whale. The oil it carried in its spongy head burned with the clearest and brightest flame anyone had ever seen. In pursuit of this valuable fuel, whaling ships went out to every ocean of the globe.

Square-rigged whaling ships were equipped with four or five whaleboats, with harpoons and lances, enormous lengths of line coiled in tubs, and with brick ovens called tryworks, for boiling down the blubber. When a whale was sighted, the call, "There she blows!" brought every man on deck, and the small boats were lowered in pursuit. When a whale was harpooned, it might "sound," plunge deep into the sea and often, with one flick of its tail, overturn the whaleboat or shatter it to splinters. Or it might run for miles, pulling the boat after it in a breakneck race known as a "Nantucket sleigh ride."

Once a whale was killed, it was hauled to the side of the ship and made fast. As the voyage went on, the men hewed or peeled off huge strips of blubber, boiled it down in the try pots and stored the oil in casks in the hold. A whaling ship did not return till it had its hold full of oil, and a man who signed for the voyage knew well that he might not see home port for three, four, or even five years.

Before the Mast

Ships from colonial shipyards carried products from every colony to England, the West Indies and the Mediterranean—tobacco and rice from the South, grains and livestock from the Middle Colonies, salted fish and lumber from New England. Shipping became a vast industry in itself, and a new merchant class grew up in cities such as Boston, New York and Philadelphia, made up of wealthy men with impressive offices, wharves and warehouses, fleets of ships, and agents in every part of the world.

Besides lumber and fish, a Yankee captain often picked up sugar and molasses in the West Indies and transported them to Europe, trading wherever he could make a profit. Frequently he sold the ship itself at a fine price and booked passage home on another ship. Yankee captains had no scruples about bringing home a cargo of slaves as a sideline, and a few merchants made fortunes by a three-stage system of slave trading. New England rum was carried to the African coast to purchase Negroes, who were taken to the West Indies and there traded for molasses which would be brought back to New England to make more rum. This ugly practice was called the Triangle Trade.

During the Revolution another profitable sideline was discovered by merchants who armed their ships to capture enemy merchant ships. These ships roamed the seas secure in the knowledge that Congress would sanction the seizure of British goods. But the high-handed seizures were also carried on in peacetime. A privateer thought himself far superior to a pirate, but to the merchant watching uneasily for any hostile sail on the horizon there was little difference—he would lose his cargo in either case. Some adventurers, like the famous Captain Kidd, began as privateers and turned pirate.

Life at sea had an irresistible lure for colonial boys. Scholars bent over their books and apprentices toiling in shops dreamed of high adven-

A sailmaker's certificate decorated with shipping and shop scenes.
(New-York Historical Society)

An early watercolor shows a whaleboat being crushed between a whale's jaw. (Whaling Museum, New Bedford, Massachusetts)

ture before the mast. Even Benjamin Franklin confessed that as a boy he longed to go to sea. Many boys ran away from farms and shops to sign as cabin boys on trading ships or whalers, and after years at sea a good many became captains, ruling their own vessels. Life was hazardous, not only from storm and treacherous rocks, but from mutiny and pirates. A boy had to stand watch on a narrow platform on a swaying mast a hundred feet above deck, or crawl far out on an icy yardarm to furl a stiff sail in a roaring wind. The crew's quarters were narrow shelves in the foul darkness of the fo'c's'le. Food and water was scarce and often rotten and teeming with weevils. Men's nerves were strained to breaking point when the ship rolled for days or weeks on end on a calm sea. New England sailors were hard men. A man who worked his way up to the rank of captain had earned the respect of every man on sea or land. But many boys had done this by the time they were eighteen or nineteen years old.

River trade, less grueling than seafaring, attracted hundreds of adventurers. Along the rivers to the sea flowed a constant stream of products. Enterprising river captains built their own boats to suit the cargoes they carried and the peculiar features of the rivers they traveled. They knew every inch of these rivers, every bend and shallow, sandbank or rapids, as well as how to strike a shrewd bargain at the end of the voyage. On the return trips up the rivers they carried all sorts of articles for inland farmers.

Wampum and Pine Tree Shillings

Little money was involved in early colonial trade. From commerce between England and the colonies all the way down to two neighbors swapping a day's labor for a bag of potatoes, all trade was carried on by barter. Raw materials sent to England were exchanged there for manufactured articles. Colonies exchanged products. Stores accepted "country produce" for the goods on their shelves. Even after the Revolution, newspapers carried advertisements offering such trades as "Two large Ox Hides to be Exchanged for Indian Corn" and "Earthern Ware to be Exchanged for Wheat, Butter and Cheese." Wages and taxes were paid in the same way. Ministers and schoolteachers received their pay in firewood and vegetables. In Fairfield, Connecticut, Madam Sarah Knight commented that the town paid part of the Parson's "sallery" with sheep's dung, which they grudged, "preferring their dung before their minister." One student is known to have paid his tuition at Harvard with "an old cow."

When the colonists first began to trade with the Indians they had to accept the current Indian coinage, which was wampum, or small polished beads made from the shells of periwinkles and clams. The blackish-purple variety, being more rare than the white, was more valuable. Presently the colonists found that wampum made a very convenient coinage for their own transactions. In 1637 it was made legal tender, six white or three purple beads equaling one penny. Strings of wampum were used for every sort of trade. However, they were not acceptable in payment of taxes—a wise provision, since the colonists before long learned to make their own beads at such a rate that wampum ceased to have any value at all.

Of course wampum had never been acceptable outside the colonies. The great desire of the colonists was to obtain money with which to trade in foreign ports. England seldom paid actual money, wanting as little as possible to leave the country. But lumber sold to the West Indies and to the Spanish colonies was paid for in silver "pieces of eight" which were much prized.

Presently the colonists took a daring step. They decided to make their own coins, a privilege which was reserved for the king and parliament alone. The first mint was set up in Boston and operated by John Hull, a silversmith. The coins he struck were at first marked with N. E. and the number of pence; later with the date, the word Massachusetts, and a picture of a pine tree. These pine tree shillings, as they were called, circulated for a number of years. Now they are museum pieces.

An early harpoon. (Whaling Museum, New Bedford, Massachusetts)

After the French and Indian wars, when there were no funds to pay the returning soldiers, the separate colonies issued paper money. Some people found paper bills convenient and liked them, but most colonists were suspicious of them, and with good reason, for their value rose and fell unpredictably. Later the Continental Congress issued such bills and they too became valueless. We still speak of something worthless as "not worth a continental."

Nails, Spoons and Bullets

Although the king was eager to encourage commerce and the development of colonial resources, he had no intention of encouraging American manufactures. Raw materials should be shipped to English factories, not made into American goods. In an attempt to protect its own industries, England tried to force the colonies to buy all their manufactured goods from England. Benjamin Franklin once protested that a colonist could

To aid in their trade, wealthy merchants set up countinghouses. (New-York Historical Society)

not make a button, a horseshoe, or a hobnail but some "sooty iron-monger or respectable buttonmaker of Britain shall bawl and squall . . ." Nevertheless, the colonists did make buttons and hobnails and a great many other necessities in ever-increasing quantity.

Lumps of bog iron had early been discovered in Massachusetts and in Connecticut. Early attempts at furnaces succeeded in melting the lumps into a soft iron but not in liquefying it. The first efficient furnace capable of turning out a good quality of iron was set up in Saugus, Massachusetts. Other furnaces were established, principally in the Salisbury district in Connecticut. There are still to be seen in these hills squat towers of crumbling stone, remains of a thriving industry. These furnaces burned charcoal, taking an alarming toll of the forests. The fire was fanned to a great heat by the use of bellows operated by water power. A good furnace could turn out eight tons of iron a week.

England was a ready market for this ore, but sooner or later the colonists were bound to tire of shipping out their iron and then buying it back again in the form of expensive manufactured goods. Blacksmiths soon began to fashion the needed articles—pots and kettles, bells for meeting houses, chains, sleigh runners, and tools of all sorts.

Many blacksmiths were true artists, adding to necessary things such as latches and weather vanes fine workmanship, interesting designs and graceful proportions. They also took pride in their ability to shoe a horse neatly, an art that required accuracy and skill. Shoeing an ox was even more of an accomplishment. Since the hoof of an ox is divided, the blacksmith had to make eight half-shoes instead of four. Moreover, the ox has small feet and cannot support his great weight on three of them. In order to shoe him, the blacksmith had to hoist him off the ground on wide straps suspended from a scaffold.

Country people made their own nails and tacks on small forges set up on their own hearths. Nails were made from long rods about a quarter of an inch thick. A farmer would heat one end of the rod at his forge, and make a point by beating it on all sides with a hammer. Then he inserted the nail in a "swage hole" on his anvil, broke the nail from the rod with a blow of hammer and chisel, and hammered it flat around the top of the hole. The cooled nail lifted easily from the hole.

Toward the middle of the eighteenth century deposits of tin were discovered, and pewter, which had been imported from England, became a popular material for tableware of all kinds. The finest pewter was composed of 80 percent tin and 20 percent copper or lead. It was a soft metal, and articles made of it wore out quickly, but it lent itself to simple and graceful designs, and housewives liked it because it could be polished to

Above: Head and tail of a Pine Tree Shilling. Until 1868 these coins, minted in Boston, were all dated 1652. Right: Issued by the Continental Congress, such bills as this one lost their value and gave rise to the expression, "Not worth a continental." (Chase Manhattan Museum of Moneys)

a gleaming luster almost like silver. Tableware was made by two processes. "Sad ware," such as plates and platters and other flat pieces, were hammered out from sheets of metal. Hollowware, such as bowls and porringers, were cast in molds. Spoon molds were often lent from house to house, and families made their own spoons or melted down and remodeled the worn-out ones. Very little colonial pewter remains today, because at the time of the Revolution families donated their tableware to be melted down into bullets.

In the last part of the eighteenth century a few men in Pennsylvania realized that there were coal deposits which could be used for fuel. Coal was already known in parts of England, but only with the greatest difficulty were Americans persuaded to try it in place of wood. The daring merchants who gambled on mining the first coal and laboriously hauling it down the mountain found it almost impossible to sell. Until a practical system of transporting it was worked out, coal remained a newfangled luxury.

Craftsmen and Clockmakers

During the eighteenth century, American cabinetmakers, mainly in New England and in Philadelphia, produced furniture that rivaled any made in England or France. There were no real factories, only small shops where joiners worked by hand, with no power tools to help them. Using not only the native cherry, maple and oak but mahogany imported from the West Indies, they designed beautiful chests, desks, beds, tables and chairs. They worked from English pattern books, following the instructions of the master furniture makers of England—Chippendale, Hepplewhite and Sheraton. They also added distinctive variations of their own. Usually they made the lines simpler, emphasizing the natural beauty of the wood, which they rubbed to a soft luster. No doubt there was also much cheap and serviceable furniture made in these little shops, but the lovely and graceful pieces which have come down to us as heirlooms were made with infinite care and skill, and decorated with fine carving.

Clocks were made in the same painstaking way. Because both metal and machinery were scarce, clockmakers fashioned the intricate wheels and plates entirely of hardwood, such as cherry or oak. A clockmaker made the parts only, working through the winter months on his clocks and in summer selling them throughout the countryside. A customer who purchased clock parts could either enclose them in a homemade case or order a cabinet from a joiner. Sometimes people simply hung the parts on the wall, with bare face and pendulums swinging, and called them "wag-on-the-walls." Gradually clockmakers began to make cases to go with their clocks, the most handsome of which were the tall standing clocks we know as grandfather clocks.

Blowing Glass

Glass windows were among the first signs of prosperity. Oiled paper might do for the first cabin, but when a man built a substantial house nothing would do but glass panes. For more than a century these had to be ordered from England. The colonists experimented with glassmaking, and early settlers at Salem and at Jamestown succeeded in making glass beads which delighted the Indians. During the first hundred years of the colonies many attempts were made to establish a glass factory. Caspar Wistar, a German colonist, and his son Richard operated a successful factory for many years in New Jersey. Another German, Heinrich Wilhelm Stiegel, who set up a glassworks in Pennsylvania, perfected a fine clear flint glass of great brilliance, molding it into bottles and goblets of blue, rose, amethyst and green. By the end of the century a number of factories were making excellent window glass, bottles and tableware.

Glassmaking required great skill and steady nerves. The molten mass, composed of sand, soda or potash, and lime from oyster shells, was melted down in a crucible, in an arched furnace of brick. The glass blower used a metal blowpipe to remove a lump of molten material from the pot. He then blew through the pipe till the lump swelled to a bubble, transferred the bubble to a metal rod, and by rolling the rod on the two arms of his workbench, molded the mass into the shape he desired, reheating it from time to time to keep it pliable. To make window glass he spun the rod between his hands till the mass widened out into a flat disk. When the disk was thin enough, he snapped off the rod, leaving a small lump of rough glass in the center which was known as "the bull's-eye." Many old houses still contain window panes with a bull's-eye, once considered a flaw but now cherished as an antique.

Left: The cooper, or barrel maker, was an increasingly important craftsman because almost all merchandise was packed in barrels.

Below: Brace and bit, dated 1785. (Southold Historical Society, Long Island)

Paper, Printing and Newspapers

The scarcity and expense of paper was a real handicap in all the colonies, particularly to the growing printing business. Paper for individuals to write on was a luxury. In the early schools pupils often learned to write on birch bark. During the Revolution General Washington had to send vital messages to his officers on torn scraps of paper. Diaries and letters written long after the war often contained double lines, made by turning the page upside down and filling in the spaces between the lines, a custom that makes old letters very taxing to modern readers' eyes.

The first paper mill in the colonies was set up by William Rittenhouse, a papermaker from Holland, at Germantown, Pennsylvania, in 1690. Benjamin Franklin, who had reason to be interested, was later instrumental in organizing a number of mills. Paper was made from linen rags, boiled down with lye to make a pulp which was dipped out into flat molds and pressed into sheets. There was always a shortage of linen, and after the Revolution the need was so great that newspapers carried notices urging people to save rags.

There were other factors to discourage early printers. Until after 1750 most of the paper, all printing presses, the type, and even the ink had to

Prints showing a saddler (far left), a buttonmaker (left), and a tinsmith, from a children's book. (Free Library of Philadelphia)

Below: Wag-on-the-wall clock. (Old Sturbridge Village)

be imported from England. The first press was set up in Cambridge, Massachusetts, and for more than thirty years was the only one in the colonies. But demand for printed material increased rapidly, and other printers set up shops in Boston. By 1690 they were putting out not only pamphlets and almanacs, but had printed a few books by American writers. Within the next hundred years American printers learned to build their own presses and construct their own type. By the Revolution printed matter of all kinds was widespread in the colonies. Philadelphia had overtaken Boston by this time and led all the colonies in the printing trade.

For the most part the publications that issued from the early presses were a steady flow of sermons and religious tracts, but one important achievement was the newspaper. In 1704, William Campbell, postmaster of Boston, who was in the best possible position to receive the latest news, formed the habit of passing it on by writing letters to his friends and sending them by the mail carriers. More and more friends began to demand these letters and even offered to pay for them. Before long Mr. Campbell had orders for more letters than he could write out by hand, so he had them printed. Thus the first newspaper was born. Other post-

*Ironworks established at Saugus,
Massachusetts, in 1650.*

masters and printers followed his example. Benjamin Franklin had his own paper in Philadelphia, and other printers soon established them in New York and Williamsburg. So great was the eagerness for news in the colonies that by the Revolution there were thirty-seven regular papers.

These early newspapers were single-folded sheets, making four pages about the size of a modern magazine. Most of the news was from England. On the first page was a reprint of the latest letter or paper which had arrived by ship—news perhaps already many weeks old, but fresh and of intense interest to the colonists. There was little colonial news other than the announcements of ships arriving and departing, and the cargo they carried.

Just as today, a good many colonists must have read the newspapers mainly for the advertisements. The little ads, which filled most of the remaining three pages, give us a fascinating picture of town life of that

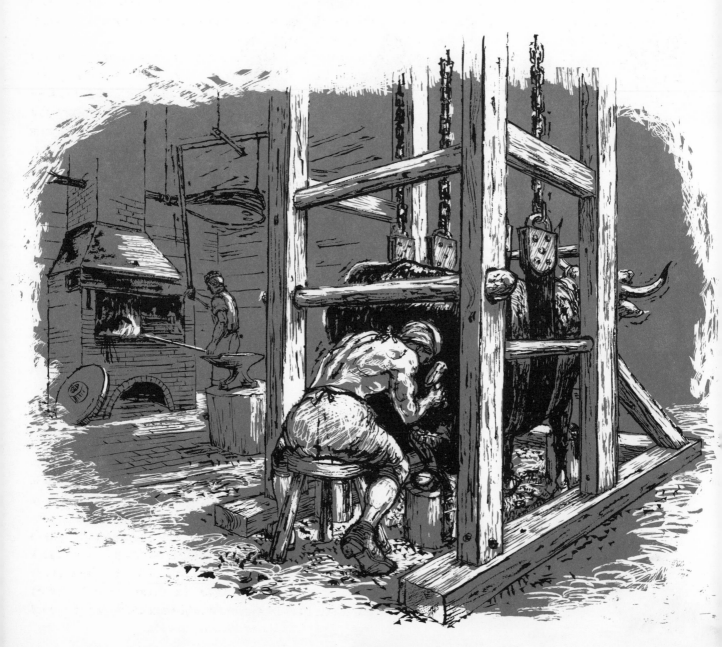

An ox shoe, made in two pieces to fit a cloven hoof. (Old Sturbridge Village)

Shoeing an ox, the blacksmith uses a sling to support the animal's great weight.

day. Stores announced an astonishing variety of goods just arrived from England—raisins, Bohea tea, snuff, nail rods, silver watches, Scotch plaids, and musical instruments, all of which would be exchanged for country produce. Wine merchants offered the finest imports. Dancing teachers, music teachers, and private schools proclaimed their superior qualifications to instruct the young. Houses and farms and horses and slaves were offered for sale. Always there were notices of horses lost, strayed, or stolen. And in every issue there were notices of runaway indentured servants or slaves, with descriptions and comments such as "wearing his master's best coat," or "having a fondness for spirits."

After the Revolution the news from England was replaced by news of the doings of Congress, and sometimes by letters from France. By this time the advertisements had spilled over to the first page. Announcements of lotteries were conspicuous now, and long columns were devoted to the winning numbers. We can imagine that these were scanned with the same breathless interest with which modern readers turn to the baseball scores and the stock market reports.

Newspapers had a far more important function than entertainment in early American life. During the Revolution they carried inspiring messages of the fate of independence to every corner of the colonies and kept alive the patriotism of remote people. In the uncertain days after the war, when the men who had framed the new Constitution were striving to win the separate states to accept it, these leaders—Jefferson, Paine, Hamilton, Jay, and others—used the newspapers to explain to people everywhere the great issues involved. Many historians believe that the newspapers made possible the rapid adoption of the Constitution.

The Rise of "King Cotton"

All colonial women knew how to spin and weave, but they longed for the smooth fine materials that the English mills provided. Weaving was England's leading industry, and all the mechanical processes were kept closely guarded secrets in the fear that America might become a rival. In America the first cloth mills were only houses in which a number of hand looms were kept operating at the same time. Machinery for weaving came to this country some time after the Revolution, and was used first not for flax or wool but for cotton.

From the time of the first settlements England had hoped to raise cotton in America. It took many years of experiment, however, to produce a cotton plant which would grow on American soil. The climate of the Northern colonies proved unsuitable, but in the Southern colonies many families managed to raise small patches on their own land. This new type of cotton had one great disadvantage. The seeds clung to the lint so tightly that they had to be removed very slowly and with great difficulty. A man working for one whole day could pick only one pound of cotton lint. An entire family working during the evenings for months could pick scarcely enough for their own clothing. The thread which the women spun from this lint was too weak to make the warp threads which stretched across the frame of the loom. It could be used only for the woof

*An early press. It could
print a newspaper only
one sheet at a time.*

threads in the shuttle, and the warp had to be made of wool or flax. Southern housewives, especially in North Carolina, made a good deal of this mixed cotton cloth for their own families, but the supply of cotton which England had hoped for was never possible.

In the last years of the eighteenth century, two inventions changed the manufacture of cotton so completely that the whole pattern of American life was destined to change with it. The first was the cotton gin, a machine for picking the seeds from the cotton, invented by Eli Whitney in 1793. The second was the Arkwright spinning frame, already in use in England but protected by the utmost secrecy. Samuel Slater, a young English mechanic, came to Providence, Rhode Island, and there set up, entirely by memory, a copy of the English machinery. With these two inventions cotton speedily became "King" in the South, and the way was paved for the industrial revolution in the North.

Those Tall Beaver Hats

Beaver skins which were shipped to England were purchased back again in the form of fashionable and costly beaver hats. Naturally the colonists soon tried their hands at this enterprise also. The hatmaking industry flourished mainly in Connecticut where it was established in Danbury, in 1780. Hats were made entirely by hand. First, workers snapped the fur pelts with catgut bow strings to remove the long hair. They then boiled the pelt in water till it was shrunk, rolled it flat, and removed the remaining hairs with tweezers. The hat they made of this tightened and matted fur was tall and bell-shaped, with a heavy rolling brim. It cost thirty-eight shillings, lasted a lifetime, and was usually passed down from father to son. Two hats a day was a good rate for one workman.

When Alexander Hamilton became the first Secretary of the Treasury in 1789, he made a survey of the manufactures in the new republic. Besides those we have mentioned he listed many others, including the making of rum, candles, pottery, copper and tin wares, snuff, lampblack and gunpowder. His report showed how rapidly industry was growing in America. But in our modern day it is difficult for us to realize how very small most of these industries actually were, and that they were carried on in "factories" which were only one-room shops. Hamilton did all that he could to encourage these small beginnings, looking forward to the time when America would no longer have to depend on foreign nations for its manufactured goods. In an age when most Americans were still farmers, he was confident that the United States would one day become a great industrial nation.

Advertisements from the Philadelphia "Federal Gazette" (New York Public Library)

By Sea and by Land

8

Today, when one can cross the American continent in a few hours, it is difficult to realize how timidly an early colonist set out on a journey of a few miles. No one in the first colonies ever traveled for pleasure. Most folks, having endured pain and weariness and terror to reach their chosen home site, rarely left it again.

In all the colonies, the earliest and the easiest way to travel was by water. First settlements everywhere were made close to the water's edge, and towns spread slowly along the shores of harbors and rivers. Visiting between settlements was done by boat. In Virginia and in Boston and New York, people often went to church or to town meeting or to visit their neighbors in small boats. Settlers who did not have boats of their own took the local ferry, which was merely a rowboat operated by an obliging man. In 1639 a passenger could be rowed from Boston to Charles-town for one penny. Folks in New Amsterdam who wanted to cross the river to Brooklyn summoned a ferryman from the field where he was farming by blowing on a horn.

The woods and forests that lay behind the settlements were filled with unknown dangers. When the first colonists explored new territory they went by water, following a coastline and venturing up rivers. They used the large vessels, the barks, brigs, brigantines and snows that had brought them across the ocean. But soon they were making smaller boats for use along the shores—shallops, and sloops and schooners. Occa-sionally they bought Indian canoes, but Englishmen were clumsy in canoes and continually tipped them over. Isaac Weld, a traveler who had to resort to a canoe to get across a river in 1796, told of spending more time in the icy water than in the canoe, and of wading waist-deep to dislodge his craft from rocks or to guide it through rapid currents.

The familiar English shallops, which were little more than rowboats equipped with sails, were not altogether dependable either. Governor Winthrop's journal is filled with sad accounts of boats overturning, and only rarely could he rejoice that a passenger had been saved.

But New Englanders took naturally to the sea, and the greater part of them made their living in fishing or trading. As ships grew larger and both fishermen and traders ventured farther out to sea, there were many tragic shipwrecks. Boston Light, the first lighthouse in the colonies, was built in 1716 with a hope of preventing some of these disasters. But in spite of faithful keepers who filled the lamps with oil two or three times a night, the slender ray did not reach far over the dangerous waters.

River boats, though safer, were unpredictable. Without a breeze to

The Long Island Ferry, from an engraving. (New-York Historical Society)

fill its sail, a boat could lie becalmed for days or even weeks. It frequently took a ship two weeks to make the five-day voyage up the Connecticut River from Saybrook to Hartford. But small trading boats were carrying goods and passengers up all the colonial rivers by 1700. There was a more-or-less regular service between such towns as Trenton and Philadelphia and New York and Albany. Later in the century, when the great movement of people into the Western territories began, whole families moved by boat, going up the Susquehanna River in Pennsylvania, and later down the Ohio. Of the many remarkable and useful boats that the pioneers developed, the most popular was the flatboat, a huge floating barge topped with a crude cabin in which a family could live en route. Endless patience and hard labor was needed for such a trip, and often all the passengers waded in shallows, poling or even dragging their boats upstream. But in spite of the dangers and frustrations of travel by boat, people preferred it to the far greater discomforts of travel by land.

"Shank's Mare"

When the first colonists ventured inland there was only one way to set out—by foot, popularly known as Shank's mare. They took the old foot-

135

paths which the Indians had followed for years, and which led over firm dry ground. The Indians had marked their trails by signs invisible to white men, so the settlers blazed them with gashes. Many four-lane highways today follow these ancient Indian trails. One of the first paths used by the settlers was the Coast Path, which ran from Boston to Plymouth. Along the famous Bay Path, from Cambridge through Massachusetts into Connecticut, the followers of Thomas Hooker, men, women and children, with cattle, swine and chickens, made the journey from Newtown to settle in Hartford in 1636. It was a two-week ordeal in the wilderness, with Hooker's ailing wife carried on a horse litter.

These blazed trails were no more than footpaths, clearings in the dense growth just wide enough for one man at a time. A fallen tree or a spring freshet could completely block the way, and men carried their hatchets as well as their muskets always in hand. Terror might lurk at any turning, for the Indians often trailed travelers for miles by parallel paths known only to themselves. There were rushing streams and steep-banked rivers. Often the greater part of the journey had to be made in wool and leather that never dried out from one stream to the next. Small wonder the settlers spoke with awe of "going abroad" when they undertook a journey of a few miles. Governor Winthrop, when he visited Governor Bradford in Plymouth, took two days to make the trip, wading through swamps and crossing the river on the back of an Indian guide.

Our ancestors were stout walkers, however, and thought nothing of hikes that would win a Boy Scout a Merit Badge today. There is a record of a baker in Portsmouth, New Hampshire, who until he was eighty years of age sometimes walked sixty-six miles in one day to purchase his flour. After arranging for shipment of the flour by boat, he walked home the next day.

In the cities fashionable men and women were carried through the streets in sedan chairs mounted on long poles and borne by servants, often Negro or Indian slaves. Governor Winthrop rode in such a chair in 1646, and a hundred and fifty years later Benjamin Franklin rode about Philadelphia in the same manner.

The hazards of travel.

Saddle and Pillion

Horses were very early shipped from England. They were most popular
in the wealthy Virginia colony, where there was more open land and
plenty of slave labor. In the North a horse was a luxury the average
farmer could not even hope to afford. In the first place, a horse cost almost
three times as much as a cow and was certainly not so useful. In the
second place, before horses could be used outside a town, the narrow
footpaths had to be widened and the settlers had all they could do to
clear their own farms.

Thrifty New Englanders devised several methods of stretching the
usefulness of one horse. The most practical arrangement for two men
traveling together was the "ride and tie" method. One man would mount
the horse and ride for an agreed distance. Then he would dismount, tie
the horse to a tree, and proceed on foot. The second man would walk to
the point where the horse waited, ride ahead, passing the first man, to the
second determined stopping place, where he in turn would tie the horse
and walk on. In this way each man had some time in the saddle, and
even the horse had short spells of rest.

Less happy, at least from the horse's point of view, was the pillion
used by women travelers. This was a cushion strapped on behind the
saddle on which the lady perched, her feet supported by a small platform
or double stirrup. A timid damsel riding home from a village dance
needed the added safety of an arm around the rider's waist. A matter-
of-fact wife could manage to do her knitting along the way. On a Sabbath
morning the family horse, who was not forbidden to labor on the Sabbath,
plodded to church carrying his master, with a small son perched on the
saddle in front of him, and his master's wife with the baby in her arms

on the pillion behind. Probably the horse, a beloved pet, minded this less than he did weekday trips to market, when he carried bulging bags loaded with anything from grain to lumber swaying from each side of the saddle.

When a horse came to a river, he knew what was expected of him, waded in resignedly, and either carried his master across or swam behind the rowboat ferry. As horses became more numerous, ferrymen had to keep up with the times, and devised wide flat barges that could accommodate both horse and rider, or even several horses on one trip. These clumsy affairs were propelled across the river in ingenious ways. Sometimes the ferryman poled them across by thrusting his pole into the river bottom and pushing on it as he walked from one end of the barge to the other. Sometimes a cable strung from shore to shore helped to guide the boat across.

While the ferryman poles the raft across the river, the rope keeps it from drifting downstream.

The coming of horses also meant that the little bridges of three or four logs that served to get a foot traveler over a narrow stream had to be made stronger and wider. Logs were laid crosswise over the supporting logs, in the same method that made a "corduroy road" over boggy stretches. Much later the colonists learned to support longer bridges on piers sunk into a river bed and to reinforce them with wooden trusses of crossed timbers. To protect the trusses from the weather the builders covered them with planks. Gradually they built both trusses and planks higher, till they covered the whole bridge with a protecting roof. But the fascinating and much-photographed covered bridges were not actually constructed till after 1800.

Riding in Style

By the end of the seventeenth century, plantation owners in the South, and prosperous gentlemen in Boston, New York and Philadelphia imported four-wheeled coaches from England. These were handsome affairs with high wheels, two wide seats which faced each other inside the carriage, and a driver's seat perched high outside. They were gaily painted in red or yellow or blue, with contrasting wheels and trim. In the eighteenth century they became more and more ornate, carved and gilded on the outside, and upholstered with blue or crimson or dove-colored cloth within. The coats of arms of the owners were emblazoned on the door panels. The harness sparkled with brass and silver bells, and both coach and horses flaunted brilliant plumes. George Washington purchased for his wife in Philadelphia an elegant chariot built in London, of cream color with gilt medallions, drawn by six horses and attended by servants in white liveries trimmed with scarlet. The four or six or even eight horses which pranced before these luxurious coaches were not merely for show —a good deal of horse power was actually needed to draw the vehicles over the atrocious roads even at three or four miles an hour. Outside the city limits a coach was useless.

Only the wealthiest could afford a coach and four. But the ordinary citizen was shortly able to ride in a coach for hire. The first public coach, a two-wheeled cart with two horses, took up its stand in front of a Boston tavern in 1712. Judge Sewall, who was quite prosperous, went courting in a hired coach, and he was scandalized when the widow he favored suggested that he should maintain one himself.

The Farmer's Chariot

Carriages and coaches were for town folks only. In the country a man who had a burden he could not carry on his back used an ox. For a farmer, a horse to ride was a luxury, but an ox was a necessity. It has been said that without oxen America could never have been settled. They helped to clear the land of rocks and trees, and made possible the roads through the wilderness. One way that the colonists paid the debts for their passages or land grants was to provide vast trunks of trees, pines as much as four feet in diameter and 200 feet high, for masts for the king's navy. As many as thirty-two yoke of oxen in a long line were needed to drag one of these masts over the rocky land to the coast.

With a homemade wagon fastened behind his ox, the farmer too had his chariot. A country oxcart was an awkward conveyance, with solid wooden wheels made from cross-sections of great trees. The cart had no springs and no covering, but it gave good service year after year, carrying the family to meeting on Sunday and a heavy load of produce to market on weekdays. An ox and wagon could make ten or thirteen, even twenty miles, in a day. In the winter, oxen were used for breaking out the town roads after a snowstorm.

Winter was the best time for transporting heavy freight. Wooden runners could slide swiftly where wheels jolted and stuck. As soon as a heavy blanket of snow covered the roads, the farmer prepared for his yearly trip to the city. Sometimes this trip was a community affair with fifty or sixty men traveling together in a long line of sleighs. A homemade pung was hitched behind the oxen and loaded with the produce that was piled up and waiting. Pork, venison, wheels of cheese, firkins of butter, bags of corn and peas and grain, homemade brooms, knitted socks, all the products of a long summer of labor were loaded in, till there was not an inch to spare and the farmer himself had to stand on a little step in the rear of the pung. His wife would have ready a good supply of food for the trip, which would take several days. The most practical form of picnic was a large bean porridge which would hang from the side of the pung and freeze solid, to be chopped off in hunks when a man was hungry. This main fare would be rounded out with thick bread and doughnuts. To be sure, there was a tavern along the way where a meal could be purchased, but a farmer liked the food he was used to, and even when he stopped for the night, he could save money by warming his own food at the tavern fire.

Jingle Bells!

In the towns the first jangle of sleighbells ushered in a season of gaiety. The Dutch colonies were enjoying sleighing parties and races as early as 1700, and it did not take New Englanders long to discover that sledges were good for something besides transporting goods. By the end of the century the crude sleds and pungs had been transformed into vehicles very like carriages, with light graceful lines and gaily painted decorations. A young English girl who visited New England wrote in her journal:

> *The pleasant custom of sleighing much contributes to enliven the country at that dreary season ... The frequent cheerful ringing of bells which are fixed to the horses of every sleigh seem quite in unison with the general gaiety around ... The sensation one feels while sliding so rapidly along is very pleasant.*

Conestoga Wagons

In the Conestoga Valley of Pennsylvania the German settlers developed a very different type of vehicle in which to carry their grain and farm produce to the coast. This was the heavy Conestoga Wagon, often twenty-four feet in length, useful to carry great loads for a long distance. The body was boat-shaped, curving upward at front and rear and outward at the sides, so that the load was kept from shifting on steep inclines. Over a framework of arches stretched a homespun covering. This was the great-grandfather of the covered wagon in which the pioneers were later to move westward.

The wagons were all painted alike, their sides brilliant blue, their trimming bright red, dramatic contrast to the billowing white canvas. They were drawn by a special breed of powerful horses, six or eight to a wagon, decked out with costly harness, ribbons and jangling bells. The driver rode the left-hand horse nearest the wagon. He was a man of authority and he had good reason to be proud of his job. His team of horses were beautifully trained. A wagon and six horses stretched to a length of sixty feet, and they traveled at a good clip, in long lines of fifty

A sedan chair, imported from England about 1750.
(Colonial Williamsburg)

to one hundred wagons at a time. What modern highways can show us any sight so thrilling as these flashing blue-and-red wagons must have been with their gaily decked horses, thundering as far as the eye could see along a Pennsylvania road?

Stagecoach Journey

Very gradually, as the roads were widened and their surfaces improved, coaches ventured outside the town limits, and finally set up services between towns. For a journey of any distance a frequent change of horses was necessary, and "stages" were set at intervals of about twelve miles where the exhausted team would halt, a fresh team would be harnessed

Only the rich could afford this elegant chair and its porters.

in its place, and the coach would lumber on again. In 1732 a stage wagon ran between Philadelphia and New York. The passengers spent a week on the way, and began and ended their journey by ferry. By 1771 an improved wagon called "The Flying Machine" was making the same trip in two days. A year later a regular stagecoach service carried passengers from Boston to New York, a trip of ten days.

From the journals of two colonial travelers we can get a vivid picture of these stagecoach journeys. Josiah Quincy told of his departure from Boston:

> *The stage left Boston at 3 o'clock a. m.; and at 2 o'clock a man was sent around to the houses of those who were booked for the passage. His instructions were to knock, pull the bell, shout and disturb the neighbors as much as possible; in order that the person who was to take the coach might be up and dressed when it reached his door. When the coach arrived, there was no light inside, and the passengers waited until daylight before they could see who were their fellow travelers.*

Jan. 23, 1793.

Five Dollars Reward,

Loſt from behind the New Line Stage Induſtry, from New York to Philadelphia, on Tueſday the 22d inſt. ſuppoſed between Germantown and this city,

A ſmall Caravan Trunk,

covered with paper and paper bordering of a different colour, containing ſundry wearing apparel, amongſt which are, a black ſattin cardinal, trimed with black lace and lined with perſian, a dark chintze petticoat, in which was a picture framed with glaſs, with the Free Maſons arms, a white muſlin petticoat, net ground, trimed with a narrow fringe, a muſlin jacket with a broad fringe, ſome ſhifts, and pairs of white ſtockings, with ſundry other things, conſiſting all of womens apparel.

N. B. Whoever has found the ſame or can give any intelligence thereof to the Printer, ſhall have the above reward.   d3t.

Right: To keep the stagecoach from over- turning, the driver would call on passengers to lean out of the windows.

Advertisement for milady's lost trunk, from the Philadelphia "Federal Gazette." (New York Public Library)

And Thomas Twining, an English traveler in 1795, described his journey in a Philadelphia mail wagon: He spent the night at a "miserable inn," had a "sparing and ill-drest repast" and at "half past two the tawny girl appeared with a candle in her hand and announced that the wagon would soon be ready."

> *The vehicle was a long car with four benches. Three of these in the interior held nine passengers, and a tenth person was seated by the side of the driver on the front bench . . . There was no space for luggage, each person being expected to stow his things as he could under his seat or legs . . . The entrance was in front, over the driver's bench. Of course the three passengers on the back seat were obliged to crawl across all the other benches to get to their places. There were no backs to the benches to support and relieve us during a rough and fatiguing journey over a newly and ill-made road . . . (We) crossed a floating bridge, two logs placed side by side and planks nailed across them; The jolt- ing of the wagon in . . . rapid descents was almost insupport- able . . . The wagon, in winding through the trees and over the*

*roads, was often so depressed in the soft ground and old ruts on
one side that the passengers were obliged to press toward each
other. Without this perpetual trimming we should certainly have
overturned.*

Stagecoach drivers were popular heroes, bold, self-confident men with an
air of high adventure. They had to be rugged to endure the heavy strain
of driving twenty miles a day over rocks and bogs, and they had to be
courageous to brave the constant danger of attack. When a driver at full
speed swept up to the door of a tavern, brought his horses to a superb
stop, tossed the reins to the groom and strode into the tavern, every eye
turned to him. Small boys dreamed of becoming stagecoach drivers,
just as today they aspire to be astronauts.

Lone Wayfarers

Men of real courage who urged their horses over the hazardous trails
were the post riders. In the early settlements the delivery of mail was
haphazard, and each town had its own method for handling important
dispatches. In 1673 a post rider began a regular mail circuit between
Boston and New York. The trip took him one week in summer and two
in winter, and the route he followed through Connecticut is still known
today as the Boston Post Road. He picked up letters at certain designated
points and delivered them to taverns along the route, where they were
thrown on a table and picked over by every passer-by. The message folded inside was protected by a glob of sealing wax, which often bore the
print of a massive seal ring. Throughout the eighteenth-century post
riders traveled between all the colonies, and local riders delivered letters from one town to another. It was not until the Continental Congress
appointed Benjamin Franklin the first Postmaster General that these
various routes were organized into a dependable service.

The post riders were courageous and conscientious men, who delivered the mail safely through winter sleet and spring flood. Certainly they
were not overpaid. A vote in the town records of Fairfield, Connecticut,
in 1712 authorized a raise in pay for the post riders who carried mail to
the surrounding towns. Henceforth they were to receive three pence a
mail, and three pence half-penny from November to April. Letters were
paid for by the receiver, not the sender, and a New Hampshire letter
carrier remembered the tricks by which the townsfolk avoided the payment. Sometimes a code was arranged and concealed in the address, so
that the receiver could look carefully at the letter and then refuse to
accept it. Since post riders also carried newspapers, and the payment on
these was lower than on letters, some folks sent their messages on the
papers themselves by circling letters and words. Post riders were expected to deliver verbal messages as well as all sorts of unwieldy pack-
ages, and they were also expected to assist lone travelers on the road.

From the earliest days there were a few men who did not like to
settle down but chose to spend their days wandering from place to place.
Such men were the peddlers. The first peddlers plodded on foot, occa-

*Before country stores,
farmers made yearly trips
to town, their produce
piled high on sleds called
pungs.*

*One of a set of wooden
bog shoes worn by horses
while harvesting
salt hay from marshes.
(Southold Historical
Society, Long Island)*

sionally on horseback, from town to town, with packs on their backs. They offered to housewives lumps of indigo dye, needles and pins, small wares, a few jokes and a bit of flattery. They expected to be invited into the kitchen for a glass of buttermilk and a piece of pie and they were not above helping the farmer in exchange for a night's lodging. The peddler had about him a hint of mysterious far-off places, and his familiar figure with its bulky pack was eagerly awaited in lonely settlements.

And every summer there were the tramps, genial, lazy men who showed up in the same towns year after year as surely as the buttercups and the locusts. One such man, named Jacquith, is said to have roamed the byways of New Hampshire for many years, accompanied by a heifer and a pig. He never refused a meal, but he had entertainment to offer in return. For five cents his heifer would jump over a pole For two cents his pig would jump over a lower pole. If folks preferred a little inspiration, for five cents he would pray, and for fifteen cents he would preach a sermon "as good as any you would hear on Sunday."

Some people seem to be born with a lively curiosity about distant places. Such a person was Sarah Kemble Knight, a woman who refused

It required six or eight horses to pull the blue and red schooner-like Conestoga wagons down the rough roads.

to be intimidated by cold or rain or lurking wolves or the gossip of her neighbors. In 1704, when few men and even fewer women ever traveled more than a short distance from where they had been born, she set out on a business journey on horseback from Boston to New York. How the neighbors must have shaken their heads over their spinning wheels at such gallivanting! Yet if she had stayed properly at home we would never have had her fascinating journal. For Madam Knight had a remarkable ability to describe what she saw, and night after night, by the light of a candle in some wretched inn, she set down the day's happenings.

For much of her journey she was under the protection of the post rider, but sometimes she had to dicker with the local farmers for a boy to guide her to the next stopping place. Even he sometimes lost his way. She set out from Boston in October when the days were shortening, and dark often overtook her before she found a place to rest. She traveled through icy rains and snows over mere footpaths. Once she recorded: "Here we found great difficulty to traveling, the way being very narrow,

and on each side the trees and bushes gave us very unpleasant welcomes with their branches and boughs, which we could not avoid, it being so exceeding dark." In another section "the roads all along this way are very bad, encumbered with rocks and mountainous passages." On one occasion her horse dropped under her. She was terrified of river crossings. Once she stood shivering for an hour on the shore of a "roaring river" before she found courage to step into the waiting canoe.

The distance from New York to Boston was then reckoned to be 274 miles, a distance which an automobile covers in about five hours. The return trip took Madam Knight ten weeks of toilsome traveling. On the windowpane of the Boston school where she taught, Madam Knight scratched these words with her diamond ring:

> *Through many toils and many frights*
> *I have returned, poor Sarah Knight.*
> *Over great rocks and many stones*
> *God has preserved from fractured bones.*

Circuit Riders

Of all those who traveled the roads of early America, those who most deserve remembrance are the circuit riders. These were evangelists, young men most of them, who rode on horseback from town to town, preaching the gospel of the Methodist Church, founded in England by John Wesley. Wesley himself spent most of his life on horseback, covering incredible distances to preach to the countryfolk of England. Following his example, his preachers did not settle in established churches, but followed a plan of itinerant preaching.

Perhaps the greatest of the circuit riders was Francis Asbury, who came to America in response to a call for volunteers. He traveled for forty-five years on foot and horseback, mainly on wilderness roads over the Allegheny Mountains. From his journal it has been estimated that he traveled 275,000 miles and preached 16,000 sermons. Another famous rider was Jesse Lee, who set out in 1789 with all New England as his circuit. In one state after another he preached, under trees, in private houses and barns, wherever people gathered to hear him.

These young preachers had a gospel that went straight to the hearts of

Left: A crowded stage-coach leaves a tavern. (New York Public Library)

Right: Some local citizens in the corner of an 18th-century tavern. (New-York Historical Society)

Below: A pewter tankard for serving ale. (Metropolitan Museum of Art)

weary, lonely settlers. Where the Puritans still thundered the fear of God, the Methodists stressed the love of God, and the value of every individual in His sight. Furthermore, they practiced what they preached, striking out wherever they went against injustice, and poverty and disease. Theirs was no easy ministry. They lived lives of great austerity. They were continually exposed to damp and cold. They preached to frontiersmen, rough-and-ready men more than willing to toss a minister out of town. They constantly needed ready wits, and sometimes ready muscles to defend themselves. In their zeal they pushed far beyond their strength, and they wore themselves out. Few itinerant preachers were able to continue longer than twelve years. Half their number died before they were thirty years old. Yet they added an inspiring chapter to the colonizing of America, pouring out their strength in service to God and to their fellow men.

At the Sign of the Green Dragon

Such an occasional traveler as Madam Knight was hard put to it to find food or shelter at night. Country homes along the way might offer hospi-

NEWS! NEWS!!

AARON OLIVER, *Poſt-Rider*,

WISHES to inform the Public, that
he has extended his Route ; and that he now
rides thro' the towns of *Troy, Pittſtown, Hooſick, Ma-
pletown*, part of *Bennington* and *Shaftſbury, Peters-
burgh, Stephentown, Greenbuſh* and *Schodack*.

All commands in his line will be received with thanks, and executed with punctuality.

He returns his ſincere thanks to his
former cuſtomers ; and intends, by unabated diligence,
to merit a continuance of their favours.

> *O'er ruggid hills, and vallies wide,*
> *He never yet has fail'd to trudge it ;*
> *As ſteady as the flowing tide,*
> *He hands about the* NORTHERN BUDGET.

June 18, 1799.

*Left: A private postman
advertises his service.
(American Antiquarian
Society)*

*Right: Public notice of a
stagecoach route. (New
York Public Library)*

tality, but outside the towns such a thing as an inn did not exist. A few houses along traveled roads were licensed as "ordinaries," and the owners received a tax exemption to eke out their scanty profits. An ordinary was nothing more than a house where one could find a corner to sleep in and could share whatever happened to be on the family table. Madam Knight, who spent many an uneasy night in ordinaries, had few compliments for her hosts. On one evening she paid sixpence for a dinner "which was only smell." She was likewise displeased with the beds she had to sleep on, but being a woman she fared far better than the average traveler, who either shared his bed with several strangers or slept on the stone floor of the main parlor.

Before many years had passed, however, inns and taverns became numerous and comfortable. By the end of the century a traveler could write, "You meet with neatness, dignity and decency, the chambers neat, the beds good, the sheets clean, supper passable, cyder, tea, punch, and all for 14 pence a head."

With the coming of the stagecoach, inns and taverns sprang up in every town and at important crossroads. They flaunted their welcome with colorful painted signs swinging before the door, bearing such good

BOSTON,
Plymouth & Sandwich
MAIL STAGE,

CONTINUES TO RUN AS FOLLOWS:

LEAVES Boston every Tuesday, Thursday, and Saturday mornings at 5 o'clock, breakfast at Leonard's, Scituate ; dine at Bradford's, Plymouth ; and arrive in Sandwich the same evening. Leaves Sandwich every Monday, Wednesday and Friday mornings ; breakfast at Bradford's, Plymouth ; dine at Leonard's, Scituate, and arrive in Boston the same evening.

Passing through Dorchester, Quincy, Wyemouth, Hingham, Scituate, Hanover, Pembroke, Duxbury, Kingston, Plymouth to Sandwich. *Fare,* from Boston to Scituate, 1 doll. 25 cts. From Boston to Plymouth, 2 dolls. 50 cts. From Boston to Sandwich, 3 dolls. 63 cts.

.N. B. Extra Carriages can be obtained of the proprietor's, at Boston and Plymouth, at short notice.— STAGE BOOKS kept at Boyden's Market-square, Boston, and at Fessendon's, Plymouth.

LEONARD & WOODWARD.

BOSTON, *November 24, 1810.*

A tavern keeper welcomes stagecoach passengers.

English names as "The Golden Lion," "The Green Dragon," "The Sign of the Orange Tree," "The Bunch of Grapes." In Revolutionary days many of the names were prudently changed to something more patriotic. The lions and crowns were hastily painted over and replaced by eagles, and a few strokes of a paintbrush transformed the hated portrait of King George into a likeness of George Washington. One innkeeper whose sign had a British lion that was hard to disguise solved the problem by painting chains around the lion!

At the door stood the innkeeper, ready with a lusty handshake. Innkeepers were famed as genial hosts. It was said of one Boston tavern keeper that it was impossible not to be merry in his presence. The keeper would usher his guests with fine ceremony into the wide, low-raftered room. A leaping fire thawed out their numb fingers and toes, and a mug of hot cider brought a warm glow of comfort. A huge roast of beef, turning slowly on the spit, its juices sizzling in the pan below, reassured them of the ample meal to come. Presently they would sit down at the long board to a feast of beef and mutton, roast chicken and turkey, baked beans and good New England brown bread, corn, doughnuts, pumpkin cake, apple dumplings and gingerbread, and strong black tea.

After the meal fresh logs would be piled on the fire, and the guests would light up their long clay pipes, make sure that their tankards were within easy reach, and settle down for a long evening of good talk. For the tavern was not only the stopping place for stagecoach passengers, but the popular meeting place of the town. Rich and poor of all trades gathered there to hear the news, discuss the weather and taxes, and endlessly debate and argue. Doubtless the taverns were the scene of many roisterous evenings. But they were also the scene of many serious and important debates in the troubled years just before the Declaration of Independence.

Colorful signs swung before every tavern door. (Old Sturbridge Village)

High Days and Holidays

9

The colonists could not only work hard but play hard as well. But in the early days of a settlement the battle against hunger and cold left little time for playing. People could not go searching for entertainment; if they were to have any at all it had to be found right where they were. So, with imagination and spirit, they sometimes managed to turn their work into fun.

Fowling Piece and Fishing Rod

Men could have the double satisfaction of being sportsmen and good providers at the same time. The American forests were a paradise for hunters. There were black bears, lynxes, panthers, wolves and wildcats to offer excitement, as well as elk and deer and countless small animals such as foxes, otters, minks, racoons, beavers and muskrats. On a boy's eighth or ninth birthday he usually received his first light "fowling piece," a long, slender flintlock rifle; and a country boy with a few hours off from school or chores would straightway be off "a-gunning" after squirrels and partridge. Boys also set traps for muskrats and woodchucks and were very skillful at catching quail in snares of braided horsehair.

By far the greatest excitement for early hunters was wolf-hunting, which has been described in Chapter Five. A less dangerous but still thrilling sport was pigeon-hunting. Flocks of two or three hundred wild pigeons migrated in the fall, darkening the sky and "sweeping the air . . . like the breath of a thundercloud." Spreading a net and lying concealed boys could catch as many as a hundred birds with one perfectly timed pull of the net rope.

As towns grew more populated and game less plentiful, town men and boys had to content themselves with turkey shoots. They paid a small sum for each shot, and the first one to draw blood took the turkey home for his dinner.

Fishing was also both a necessity and a sport. New Englanders especially have always been ardent fishermen. The preacher, Lyman Beecher, writing of his boyhood in the 1780's, recalled with delight the moment when an uncle first put a line and hook into his hand. His daughter Catherine remembered his taking her brothers out for a holiday and returning at dusk with a whole cartload of eels.

Huskings and Quiltings

In the chapter on New England life we have already told of the custom of combining work and fun. When there was a job to be done, a plot to

be cleared of stumps and stones, a house to be raised, the neighbors rallied round and did the work together. The man whose house walls were going up provided one or two hogsheads of cider or rum, his wife set out a board laden with pies and cakes, and a rousing time was had by everybody.

In the autumn there were corn-huskings. Young people gathered in some lantern-lighted barn around a huge pile of new-picked corn for an evening of hard work enlivened by boisterous frolicking and forfeits. The lucky huckster who stripped a red ear could claim a kiss, but the one who found himself holding a black ear had his face smudged with lampblack. There were also apple-paring parties, at which barrels of apples for sauce and drying were peeled and sliced to the accompaniment of songs and stories. A girl who threw a long curling peel over her shoulder might learn the initial of her future husband. And in the early spring, in Vermont, New Hampshire and Maine, there were—and still are—sugaring-off parties, where children stuffed themselves on sticky globs of maple syrup cooled in the snow.

Women varied the monotonous and lonely tasks of the household with their own "bees." The most popular were the quilting parties de-

Captive pigeons, their feet tied, serve as decoys to draw clouds of passenger pigeons down to the nets.

scribed earlier. There is a story told of a little girl in Vermont who was so eager for a party that on a sudden impulse she invited her whole district school to a quilting, and then forgot all about it. A week later, her mother, busy about the house, was astonished to see a crowd of girls, and boys as well, storming her gate. But country women were accustomed to emergencies. She assigned an older brother to keep the boys amused in fields and barn. She hastily improvised a "quilt" from two sheets and a store of new wool. While the young quilters set to work with their needles, she called in a neighbor to help fill the oven. When the white quilt was finished, a feast of new-baked doughnuts and cookies was waiting, and the workers departed well satisfied, never knowing that they had come to an impromptu party.

In the Southern colonies such bees were unknown. Plantations were too far apart for neighborly co-operation, and it was not needed with slaves and servants to do the work. Southern neighborliness showed in the lavish hospitality that made an occasion for a feast out of any chance arrival. When invitations went out to a party, guests traveled many miles and arrived with trunks and boxes, expecting to remain for days if not for weeks.

Ninepins, Dancing and Cards

When neighbors got together, or young people had a few moments off from chores and study, what were the games they played? Stoolball is one of the earliest mentioned, and seems to have been a game with wickets, perhaps a simple form of the game of cricket which later became the national sport of England. Bowling at ninepins, quoits, shuffleboard, ball and bat, and a rowdy form of football were also popular. Most of these games were expressly forbidden in early New England. But in spite of laws, they flourished, especially in tavern yards where men and boys liked to gather.

DANCING SCHOOL.

James Robardet, refpectfully informs the Ladies and Gentlemen of Philadelphia, that his Dancing School is opened for the inftruction of young Ladies and Gentlemen, in Walnut ftreet between Third and Fourth ftreets —Hours of tuition will be made known at his School Room which will not interfere with the hours at other places of education. Hours of tuition for young gentlemen will be, from fix o'clock in the evening till feven. Gentlemen more advanced in age from feven till nine.

Any commands addreffed to him at Mr. Oeller's will be punctually attended to.

A practifing Ball will be given every fortnight at Mr. Oellers's Hotel, for the improvements of his pupils, when their parents will be gratefully admitted which will commence on Saturday the 8th inftant, A collection of new country dances and cotilions of his own compofition, will be danced at his Schooland a practifing Balls

December 4th, 1792.   mw&ftf.

In cities, dancing lessons were an essential part of polite education, from the Philadelphia "Federal Gazette." (New York Public Library)

Children of well-to-do families practising the minuet.

Card-playing, regarded with horror by the Puritans, was a common pastime everywhere. In spite of fines and prohibitions, hundreds of packs of cards arrived with every ship from England, and found eager buyers, though, even after the Revolution, there was a fine of seven dollars for selling a pack of cards. Cards, next to horse racing, were the favorite diversion of Southern gentlemen, and gambling for high stakes was common even among the poorest farmers and Negro slaves.

And the colonists loved to dance. Only the consciences of strict Massachusetts Puritans and Philadelphia Quakers forbade this pastime. Everyone else enjoyed it from the earliest days, at weddings, house-raisings, at all sorts of celebrations, even the ordaining of new ministers. Country people loved the strenuous old dances done to "step tunes," such as Old Father George, High Betty Martin, and the Rolling Horn-pipes. Every village had its local fiddler, and neighbors gathered to dance on the hard earth floors of cabins or barns. Country taverns provided ideal dancing places, and often the great hall of a tavern had a built-in fiddler's seat. Many a night, after the tables had been pushed against the wall, the rafters echoed with the stamp of feet. Very gradually even New

England relaxed its stern attitude and allowed its young folks to dance.

In the cities dancing was much more formal. Dancing masters were important members of city society, and little boys and girls learned to dance the minuet, to bow and curtsy, as seriously as they learned their reading and arithmetic. British officers were responsible for much of the gaiety of the cities, and the Church of England folk who surrounded the royal governors in Boston and New York gave elaborate balls which began at six in the evening and lasted till three in the morning. In the South, of course, there was never a ban on dancing, and the cities of Williamsburg and Charleston were renowned for the brilliance and beauty of their balls. General Washington, who must have caused a flurry among the ladies, was once known to have "danced upwards of three hours without once sitting down."

Outdoor sports flourished best in winter when the frozen lakes and rivers made getting about both easy and exciting. For some reason the Puritans who forbade little boys to go swimming on hot summer days did not frown on skating, perhaps because so many of them had become used to the sight in Holland. At any rate, the English colonists were soon copying their Dutch neighbors and skimming over the ponds and rivers.

Madam Knight, in 1704, wrote of the gay sleighing parties she saw in New York. Before the century was out, New Englanders also were writing of the joys of swift dashes over the snow, followed by supper parties.

When snow covered the rutted roads, sleighs made traveling swift and pleasant.

The First Holidays

The first holiday which has come down in history is the famous first Thanksgiving of the Plymouth colony. The custom of setting aside a day for giving thanks was an ancient one, and every colony proclaimed such a day whenever they had good reason to be in a thankful mood. Gratitude for an abundant harvest was the most frequent occasion for celebration, and gradually the November holiday became an American custom. In the early days colonists took the observance rather casually, even when it was proclaimed by the governor. There is a story told in Colchester, Connecticut, of how the townsfolk once postponed their celebration for a week in order to wait for an expected hogshead of molasses to arrive by boat from New York. For how could any family observe the holiday properly without a batch of pies?

December 25th went by almost unnoticed in the colonies. It is hard for us to realize that our Christmas festivities are quite recent in origin.

*Fun on a frozen pond included not only skating but whipping a top.
(New-York Historical Society)*

*Early skates had steel
runners but the soles
were made of wood.
(Colonial Williamsburg)*

Christmas had become such a rowdy and sacrilegious holiday in England that the Puritans were determined to ignore it altogether. The General Court of Massachusetts passed a law forbidding any observance of the day, and Judge Sewall noted in his diary for December 25th, 1685, that "the carts do come to town and shops open as usual." But with the coming of the royal governor the following year the King's Chapel in Boston held Christmas services. For nearly two hundred years New England was to be divided about this day. As Episcopal churches rose in New England towns, Congregational children heard snatches of carols and peered wistfully in at candlelit chapels they were forbidden to enter. Gradually the customs of many colonies began to cluster around December 25th. The Moravian Germans at Bethlehem, Pennsylvania, celebrated Christmas Eve by marching into a stable, singing an old carol. The custom of the New York English of exchanging presents on New Year's Day gradually shifted to Christmas. Saint Nicholas, for whom little German and Dutch children used to leave shoes or stockings to be filled on December 6th, did not become the Santa Claus of American children till after 1800.

The nearest thing to a real holiday in the early colonies was Training Day, also called Muster Day. Up till the rebellious days just before the Revolution, the king's birthday was a fine excuse for a muster, a celebration, or an "illumination" in the evening, which meant an extravagant burning of candles or oil lamps in windows and streets. After George

Washington became president, his birthday was often observed in the same way.

Colonial boys, especially in New York, had a special fondness for an English holiday on November 5th, Guy Fawkes Day. Fawkes was an English traitor who conspired to blow up Parliament in a "gunpowder plot," fortunately discovered in time. Englishmen celebrated the rescue by burning stuffed effigies of Guy Fawkes. American boys probably knew or cared little about the ancient conspiracy. To them it was a day much like a modern Halloween. They paraded through the streets in outlandish costumes, burned effigies of anyone who happened to be out of favor, and played all sorts of pranks on their exasperated neighbors.

New Englanders made holidays out of their elections. In fact, Madam Knight, on her trip through Connecticut, observed that "their chief Red Letter day is St. Election." Celebration frequently went on for nearly a week, marked by lavish consumption of "'Lection Cake, a rich fruit cake, and 'Lection beer."

The Dutch had no Puritan scruples about enjoying themselves. Their merrymaking was contagious, and many of their customs, like the New Year's visiting, were adopted by their English neighbors. But the Dutch maypole on May Day was one custom the Puritans could never tolerate. The Dutch also had Pinkster Day, celebrating Pentecost, an occasion for visiting, schnapps and games. The slaves in Albany had their own version of this holiday, and danced in African dress to the beat of eel-pot drums. Pennsylvania had Tammany Day, and the Southern Colonies celebrated with feasting and speechmaking many of the old British name days— St. Andrew, St. Patrick, St. David and St. George.

The Declaration of Independence established the first truly American holiday. On July 3rd, 1776, John Adams wrote to his wife:

> *The second day of July, 1776, will be the most memorable epoch in the history of America. I am apt to believe that it will be celebrated by succeeding generations as the great anniversary festival. It ought to be commemorated as the day of deliverance, by solemn acts of devotion to God Almighty. It ought to be solemnized with pomp and parade, with shows, games, sports, guns, bells, bonfires, and illuminations, from one end of this continent to the other, from this time foreward forever more.*

A year later Adams saw his prophecy come true, and described for his daughter the first celebration held in Philadelphia. On July 2nd, 1777, bells rang all day long. The warships on the river were decked with flags and each fired a salute of thirteen guns. In the streets soldiers continually fired volleys. In the evening there was a parade followed by bonfires and fireworks. One year later an even more elaborate celebration took place,

74   COBWEBS TO CATCH FLIES.

boys saw some children tossed about in a Toss-about.

They were singing merrily the old nurse's ditty:

"Now we go up, up, up,
"Now we go down, down, down,
"Now we go backward and forward,
"Now we go round, round, round."

The voices sounded pleasantly to *Ned's* ear; his heart danced to the notes; jumping, he called to his brother *James*, "Dear *James!* look! if I thought our mamma would like it, I would ride so."

An early "ferris wheel" from a country fair. (New York Public Library)

but this time on July 4th, the day when the Declaration had been formally adopted.

Come to the Fair!

Throughout the eighteenth century, while New England still clung to its Puritan soberness, the Middle and Southern Colonies reveled in sports of all kinds. Most popular were the country fairs. These fairs originated when farmers gathered once a year to trade livestock and farm produce. Presently they became boisterous celebrations with races and exhibitions of skill, and entertainment for three days at a stretch. Men and boys competed in running races, obstacle races, wrestling and cudgeling bouts. Sometimes even women and girls raced each other. Old and young enjoyed ridiculous contests such as grinning or whistling matches, with tobacco or plum puddings for prizes. Puppet shows, fortunetelling, and tightrope walkers amused happy crowds, and occasionally there was a traveling showman with a trained bear or lion.

Some of the colonists' ideas of entertainment were not so harmless. They had brought with them from England many rough and cruel customs. Some people thought there was no better sport than a bear- or wolf-baiting, in which the wild animal was tied to a stake and tormented by dogs. A Dutch sport which young men greatly enjoyed was riding at full speed and trying to catch a swinging greased goose. Another variation was running after a pig with a greased tail. Cockfighting, a fierce and bloody sport, delighted colonists everywhere. Southern newspapers ran advertisements of important matches featuring the names of famous fighting cocks, and a bout between two champions was sure to draw crowds from a long distance. Such amusements were not confined to fairs, but were weekly spectacles in towns and cities. In an age when a public hanging was still the greatest spectacle of all, few consciences were troubled by the sufferings of animals.

Wealthy colonists in New York and Virginia brought from England

Traveling acrobats and animal trainers brought popular entertainment to country towns. (New York Public Library)

Tightrope walkers and puppet shows were a favorite part of country fairs, especially in the South.

the ancient sport of fox-hunting. They imported splendid horses, guns and riding habits—and they even imported the foxes. George Washington had in his stables the finest horses and hunting dogs, and once wrote in his diary of hunting six days in one week. Horse racing, already known as the "sport of kings" in England, was also introduced into Virginia. Williamsburg was the scene of many a famous race. On plantations the breeding and racing of fine horses became an increasingly important feature of life. Unlike cockfighting, horse racing was exclusively the privilege of the gentry, and a tailor was once fined for presuming to match horses with a gentleman.

When the English took over the colony of New Amsterdam they discovered that the flat grassy plains of Long Island were ideal for this sport, and from that time racing developed rapidly in the North. New York newspapers of the eighteenth century devoted much space to notices of races. On fine days throngs of carriages carried New Yorkers across the Brooklyn Ferry to Hempstead to watch as many as a thousand horses compete. Races were also held in New Jersey, Pennsylvania and occasionally, though many people disapproved, in Massachusetts and Rhode Island. In Connecticut they were forbidden by law.

Though New Englanders did not encourage such a waste of time as a country fair or a horse race, they were not above flocking out to see a traveling exhibit whenever one passed through the town. Strange and wondrous animals appeared from time to time in the eighteenth century—a lion, a camel, a large white bear from Greenland, and a large baboon, "the most curious animal of its kind ever seen in America."

One of the most thrilling spectacles was the exhibition of the new French discovery, the aerial balloon. The thought of a man actually sailing through the air was so wondrous that huge crowds gathered and stood for hours gazing into the sky at the miraculous drifting ball.

Strait-laced New Englanders also indulged themselves in a form of gambling known as the lottery. This was a favorite method of raising money for churches, schools, public buildings and roads, in fact for almost any public need. Whole pages of eighteenth-century newspapers are devoted to announcements of lotteries and lists of winning numbers.

Do Re Mi

From the very beginning music gave pleasure to the colonists, even though it might be only from the jew's-harps they could carry in their pockets, or the folk songs they remembered from the Old World. The art of music flourished first in the South, where there was wealth and leisure. The spinets that graced the drawing rooms of the fine plantation houses were not for decoration only. All young ladies and most young gentlemen were expected to learn to play some instrument with skill. George Washington played a flute, and Thomas Jefferson a violoncello. Even the slaves had their own musical entertainment, liking best a stringed instrument they had brought with them from Africa, which later developed into the banjo. Negroes had a natural talent for instruments such as violins and trumpets, and they often furnished entertainment for their masters' guests.

Some of the most beautiful music in early America originated in the small German settlements of Pennsylvania. For these intensely religious people, music was a vital part of worship. At Ephrata the Palatines sang choral music in five or seven parts, and composed hundreds of melodious hymns. The Moravians at Bethlehem used trombones as their first sacred instruments, and in 1757 constructed a fine organ for their Bell House. They also had the first symphony orchestra in America and brought to this country the music of Haydn and Mozart.

Public concerts began in the South and in New York and Philadelphia early in the 1700's. Charleston boasted the first known performance of an opera in America.

M. Blanchard's
FORTY-FIFTH AERIAL FLIGHT
Is positively fixed for Wednesday, January 9th, in the Prison Court, at 10 in the morning precisely, *weather permitting.*

Those who have subscribed on the blank subscription cards distributed thro' the city, are requested to end them to Oeller's Hotel, and those who wish to subscribe, may apply at the same place, until the 3d of January inclusively. Price of subscription, Five Dollars.
December 26.   mw&ftf

As early as 1793, balloon flights caused great excitement.
(New York Public Library)

We Boys Puting up A Swing, on A large white oak tree, In the Woods of Peter Streber, formerly Susan Spangler Plantation, one mile from town; To leab and Skip by Swinging, William Streber, Lewis Miller, John Rouse, Daniel Baumgardner, Jacob Stroman, Henry Craver, Samuel aweiser. In the year—1812.

Lewis Miller, a Pennsylvania carpenter, recalls a scene from his boyhood. (The Historical Society of York County, York, Pennsylvania)

Boston, destined to become a great musical center, was slow to surrender to music. Faneuil Hall was the scene of occasional concerts for the benefit of the poor, but the fact that these concerts were usually followed by balls shows that the concertgoers were Church of England people. Puritan New England clung to its tuneless psalm-singing. Most congregations could sing by memory only three or four tunes. Not only did different churches sing them differently, so did members of the same church, all at once, each member arriving at the last note in his own due time.

Presently even Puritan ministers began to be dismayed at the singing in their churches. In 1714 John Tufts of Harvard published *A Very Plain and Easy Introduction to the Singing of Psalm Tunes*. Immediately violent arguments split church congregations apart. The old way was good enough. Notes were too hard to learn—their very names had a heathen sound! But young people seized on the hymnbook with joy. Here was a new kind of entertainment. Singing societies sprang up in every town, and singing masters—usually the dancing masters as well—organized classes for young ladies and gentlemen. Eventually the singers were allowed to sit together in the meeting-house gallery, and so the New England church choir was born.

It was only another step to the installing of pipe organs, and by Revolutionary times these were manufactured in this country. One feature of pipe organs which we forget in these days of electricity was that they depended not only on the player but also on the organblower, who had to pump unceasingly on the two handles in the rear. For every young person who learned to play one of these instruments, some obliging brother or sister had to toil through the hours of practice to keep up the wind.

By the end of the eighteenth century little boys and girls everywhere were industriously practicing their scales. Imported violins, flutes and French horns were fashionable. Always popular were the forerunners of the piano—spinets and harpsichords, in which the strings were plucked by little quills when the notes were struck. About this time their place

Grand Rehearsal of the Anniversary Ode.

Singing and music societies were a favorite form of entertainment. (Johns Hopkins University Library)

was taken by a new invention, the pianoforte, in which the strings were struck by small hammers.

Footlights and Bookworms

Of all public amusements the theater had the greatest difficulty in getting a start in America. The Puritans were not the only ones who thought that plays and actors were the agents of Satan. Even Virginia at first banned actors because "we resolve to suffer no idle persons in Virginia." It was in the Southern Colonies, however, with their tolerant disposition, that players first found welcome. Bands of traveling actors moved about, giving their plays in taverns, in court chambers and in barns, till in 1716 a combination dancing academy and theater was built in Williamsburg, and a second soon after in Charleston.

Strolling players occasionally invaded the colonies further north. By 1750 New Yorkers were enjoying performances of Shakespeare and other popular English playwrights. The Quaker stronghold of Philadelphia surrendered soon after. It was necessary to reassure the public repeatedly that plays were proper and moral. Names such as *The Fair Penitent* and *The Orphan* had a righteous sound, and sometimes even the plays of Shakespeare were disguised by such titles. *Hamlet* was once advertised as *Filial Piety*.

Towns throughout New England kept their door tight shut against such evil. Josiah Quincy, on a visit to the South, was amazed to learn that George Washington frequently attended the theater, and that even the most respectable ladies were in the audience. Such a thing would not occur in New England till long after the Revolution. Against its will, Boston had a theater during the days when British soldiers were quartered there, for the generals took over Faneuil Hall and converted it into a theater for their own amusement. Perhaps a few patriots also enjoyed a peek, for when the soldiers departed, Boston built its first real theater, with three rows of boxes.

Colonial theatergoers had to put up with many inconveniences. There were no reserved seats; servants were sent hours ahead to hold places for their masters. There were no stoves in winter, and the candles in the chandeliers dripped wax on the audience below. Privileged spectators were allowed to sit on the stage, and their comments distracted the performers. Hoodlums in the galleries hissed the actors and threw apples, sometimes even rotten eggs, onto stage and audience.

People whose favorite pastime was reading must have felt sadly frustrated in the early colonies, because a book was a rarity. Wealthy men, of course, ordered books from England, and could enjoy novels, books of travel, philosophy and poetry. Scholars and ministers collected their own private libraries of theological works. But the ordinary family was fortunate if it owned any book at all besides the Bible.

Printing presses, set up very early in Boston, remained strictly in the control of Puritan leaders, so that all they could offer to eager bookworms was a steady diet of religious pamphlets, sermons and religious poetry. These were widely sold and greatly enjoyed by hungry readers. Paper was

Playing cards often showed historical figures. In this deck, engraved about 1800, George Washington is the King of Hearts, whereas Joseph Brant, much-dreaded Indian chief, is the Knave (later called Jack) of Clubs. (Guy de Lagerberg Collection)

In New York in 1767, people went to the theatre as much to stare at the fashionable audience as to watch the players.

costly, and a man who wanted to have his writings published had to find someone, usually a group of subscribers, to finance the printing. Churches often voted the money to pay for printing their minister's sermons. One man, who owned a woolen mill, made a generous donation toward the publication of a book of poems, but he did so on one condition: the book must include instructions for preparing the wool sent to him!

In addition to the occasional printing of some popular English book, Boston printers issued a few lively bestsellers of narratives by men and women who had been captured by the Indians and lived to tell their tales. One of the most popular was *A Narrative of the Captivity, Sufferings and Removes of Mrs. Mary Rowlandson, who was taken prisoner by the Indians with several others and treated in the most barbarous and cruel manner by those vile savages, with many other remarkable events during her travels.*

Probably the favorite reading of every colonial family was the almanac. This little booklet, which hung from a peg near every fireplace, was consulted on all occasions, for it contained all sorts of useful facts and figures. There were weather predictions, hours of sunrise and sunset, eclipses of the sun, schedules of post riders and coaches, in addition to bits of verse, recipes, jokes and sage advice. Almost every printer issued his own almanac and gave free rein to his own imagination and talent. Benjamin Franklin is no doubt the most famous.

Franklin is also credited with the first "public library," though its public was limited. In 1728 his club of artisans and traders in Philadelphia voted to purchase books and to share them with each other. They paid annual dues, and they called their collection a social library. This idea appealed to people everywhere. In the next fifty years social libraries spread rapidly, not only in cities but in small towns. Though they were not at first actually public, it was not many years before these libraries opened their doors to all booklovers free of charge.

Like the patchwork quilts which colonial ladies stitched with pride, the life of early America, as we look back, is made up of many pieces, some somber, some gay, each small piece having its place in the intricate and varied pattern we call our American way of life. All the pieces of this gigantic quilt could never be contained in one volume. We have been able to look closely at only a few, and to see how some were old and worn, brought from England and Europe by men and women who clung to the ways they had known and loved, and how others were new and daring, invented to meet the challenge of the new world. There is a story behind every bright-colored and strangely shaped piece—a story that will reward the reader who searches for it.

And the people we have glimpsed in these pages are only a few of all who played their part in the founding of our nation. There is a story in the life of every pioneer who with hope and courage made the hazardous journey through the wilderness and with unsparing toil established a home for his family. Most of these stories were never recorded. We can only try to imagine what they might have been as we look at a battered pewter cup, an ancient musket, or a hand-carved wooden doll. But from the few true-life accounts that remain for us, in faded writing on yellowed pages, we have learned much about life three hundred years ago. To read such stories is to understand better the America we know today.

This book has been only a beginning. To you, the reader, remains the fun of searching out for yourself the story behind the special corner of America in which you live.

Index

CREDITS

All photographic sources are given beneath the illustrations. In the case of The Metropolitan Museum of Art, New York, the following additional information is given: p. 20 — Bequest of Mary Clark Thompson, 1924; p. 30 — Gift of J. Pierpont Morgan, 1927; pp. 48–9 Bequest of A. T. Clearwater, 1933; p. 52 — Bequest of Charles Allen Munn, 1924; p. 65 — Gift of Mrs. Robert W. de Forest, 1933; p. 78 — Gift of Mrs. Russell Sage, 1909; p. 149 — Gift of Mrs. J. Insley Blair, 1940, in memory of J. Insley Blair.